sweet

In memory of Gran,
whose pastry was legendary

alexina
anatole

sweet

 SQUARE PEG

project editor Emily Preece-Morrison

design Evi-O.Studio | Eloise Myatt, Evi O.

photography Yuki Sugiura

portrait photography Danika Magdalena

food styling Holly Cochrane

props styling Max Robinson

contents

introduction

never
too much

Most key life events are accompanied by something sweet: from candlelit birthday cakes to Christmas mince pies, and from multi-tiered wedding creations to cupcakes at a baby shower, sugar is the taste of celebration. And sweetness – unlike bitterness (the subject of my first book) – needs no introduction . . . the world loves sugar! It's the third most valuable crop globally, and most households will have a bag in their cupboard. The act of baking is popular, too – it's a chance to retreat to the kitchen and produce something that will be received with happiness and excitement. Even if you're not a keen baker, there will probably come a time when you have to bake *something* – such is the extent that sweet things are ingrained into our lives. This book is for you. And it's also for the hardcore dessert fans out there. Essentially, I'm saying this book is for (almost) everyone.

That being said – and in the spirit of complete honesty – there's something you should know upfront: I am anti-buttercream (do not gift me a cupcake, ever), lukewarm about meringue (the *merveilleux* cakes on page 84 changed my mind, though) and have a complicated relationship with pears (one of the lowest-acidity fruits out there). I am very much a 'leave-room-for-dessert' kind of person, but one-note flavour and bland sweetness are not for me. What *is* for me is bitter chocolate alongside vanilla-scented Chantilly (page 146); sharp raspberries against tangy sour cream (page 154); and creamy rice pudding balanced by sweet-sour sumac strawberries (page 93). Said another way: I'm drawn to desserts that have interest, that balance contrast and comfort.

This is not a book aimed at pastry chefs. I am a keen baker but an impatient technician, so most of these recipes give you maximum flavour for low effort. Take what I say next with a fat grain of salt, but aspiring to master pastry technique over all else can lead the home baker astray. There is a line to tread: you need enough basic technique to have the confidence that when you bake

a cake or a tart, or make a dough, it's going to, you know, work. At the same time, great technique does not make a cake or dessert delicious. There's a lot of style over substance out there, and I know I'm not the only one who has sampled cakes and desserts that have *looked* beautiful but tasted . . . average? Underwhelming? Cloying? Too sweet? It's a disappointing moment. Not in these pages, though: these recipes rely on creative flavours over complex techniques, and taste-wise, the focus is on balance. Which is to say that sourness, bitterness, salt and umami are welcome here.

This cookbook is a blueprint for knockout desserts and bakes, sharing my dessert 'philosophy' through ten chapters, covering a range of sweet ingredients as well as touching on the value of sweetness in savoury contexts. My focus, as ever, is on flavour, accompanied by information – be it scientific, historical or sociological – that is relevant and interesting (never boring). At the core of this cookbook are more than 80 recipes that bring the party without the fuss, so that you can indulge that sweet tooth, safe in the knowledge that none of it will be *too much*, but, instead, just right.

a brief + bittersweet history

Sugar may have a bad health rep these days but the truth is that the world operates on the stuff – without it we would die. Human brains are fuelled by glucose, just as the global economy is fuelled by sucrose (the world's third most valuable crop). We consume sugar as babies (in the form of lactose in breast milk or formula) and we never really lose the taste for it, even though our palates develop and change as we age. Sugar – with its sparkling, diamond-like crystals (or 'white gold' as the Egyptians used to refer to it) – keeps the earth spinning, but it's also at the heart of why we live in such an unequal world today.

The story of sugar really starts with honey, a liquid sweetener that was key to the development of humans. It's hard to imagine it now, because honey is firmly secondary to sugar, but when crystallised sugar first arrived in the West, it was repeatedly described as 'a kind of coalesced honey' (since honey had been the main sweetener up until that point). But where honey comes from bees, white sugar crystals come from sugar cane: a grass first domesticated by the indigenous people of New Guinea as early as 8,000 BC. It's a plant that made its way through Indonesia and Southeast Asia to India, where it got its name ('sugar' comes from the Sanskrit word sarkara, originally meaning 'grit' or 'gravel'). The sweet part of the sugar cane is its juice, which, though delicious, is an impractical and perishable product. It wasn't until the Indians worked out how to turn the sugar into jaggery, and then into crudely refined sugar crystals, that sugar's potential expanded. This crystallised sugar was called khanda (a precursor to the word 'candy'), and from here it spread both east and west: east to China, via Buddhist monks, and west across the medieval Islamic world, catalysed by Alexander the Great's invasion of India in 327 BC. When one of his officers wrote about 'a reed in India that brings forth honey without the help of bees', he was talking about sugar cane, and by the first century AD sugar had become established in the Middle East and Arabia.

But before a spoonful of sugar was used to 'help the medicine go down', sugar was considered the medicine itself: not only did it make its way into Ayurveda, the ancient Indian system of medicine, but as it moved west it was used as a treatment for fevers, coughs, stomach diseases and more, with its virtues extolled by Greek physicians, as well as the Roman author Pliny the Elder. Only the very rich used it in food, so it wasn't until the seventh century, when the Arabs started spreading the art of sugar refining across the Mediterranean, that taste became sugar's primary selling point.

Sugar made its way into Europe through invasions and wars: in the seventh century, the Arab conquest of Iberia saw sugar refineries built in North Africa and Spain, while the Crusades of the eleventh century saw samples of sugar returned to the crusaders' homelands and called 'sweet salt'. Amid the tensions between Christianity and Islam, Cyprus became a key source of production, while the trading of sugar eventually fell under the control of history's great merchant power: Venice. In the early fourteenth century, there are records of a Venetian trader bringing 100,000 pounds of sugar into the Port of London in 1319 and pricing it at 2 shillings per pound (the average worker made 40 shillings a year . . . you do the maths). Sugar was not for the masses at this point – it became a symbol of social prestige flaunted by the wealthy. In French courts, for example, audacious sugar sculptures (ironically called 'sugar subtleties') were used to mark intervals between banquet courses at royal feasts – edible art, if you like.

Sugar was rarely mentioned in Chaucer's fourteenth-century writings, but by the time Shakespeare was crafting his plays in the fifteenth century sugar featured repeatedly; it was at this point that it transitioned from luxury to staple. At this time Christopher Columbus took sugar cane over to the Americas and, driven by the growing appetite for the sweetener[1], large areas of Brazil, Suriname and the Caribbean were converted into sugar plantations. An intensive crop to grow, sugar marked the death of the indigenous people of the Caribbean (who were extinct just 100 years into the sugar trade) and the start of the Atlantic Slave Trade. In 1501, the first enslaved Africans landed and 350 years of this trade ensued, through to 1850. About 13,000,000 people were transported across the Atlantic; 25% died on the way and many more died after. It became an enduring and tortuous circuit of slavery, money and power. Slavery made sugar cheaper, which encouraged its use, including in the bitter tea and coffee that became popular in the eighteenth century. The human predisposition for sugar – previously only sated occasionally in the form of honey and ripe fruits – was encouraged by its increasing availability. Between 1704 and 1901, Britain's annual per capita consumption went from 2kg to 41kg, and by the time the Industrial Revolution came around sugar provided a fifth of workers' calories.

The British monarchy had a stake in the sugar industry (and slavery) from the beginning – right up to the nineteenth century and the reign of George III. Britain and 'the crown' were built on slavery, accounting for nearly 50% of the Africans who were enslaved, even as Spain,

---

1 One of the tropical 'drug foods', according to Sidney Mintz, author of Sweetness and Power.

Portugal, France and Belgium carried out similar human rights abuses. The sugar businesses in Barbados, Saint Dominique and Jamaica were hugely profitable and created great wealth for Britain. Meanwhile, protected prices for West Indian sugar made slave owners ruthless: they didn't need to worry about their workers – they could replace anyone they worked to death.

The Slavery Abolition Act was voted for and signed in 1833, but (according to the historian Ana Lucia Araujo): 'To this day no former slave society in the Americas . . . former slaves or their descendants . . . no African nation (have) ever obtained any form of reparations for the Atlantic slave trade.' Britain and its empire were underwritten by the sugar industry and the slavery that fuelled it. Capitalism and racism were co-created at this time and remain symbiotic to this day as mutually reinforcing structures of white supremacy (British slave owners received reparations for the loss of slaves right up to 2015). The sugar industry was worth over £67 billion in 2021 – but many, many millions paid the price.

ur evolving
sweet tooth

Sometimes, I can be a little dramatic. In *Bitter*, I claimed that my sweet tooth had died a sudden death in Paris. What I really meant was that it changed significantly; it was at this point that I stopped being able to indulge in desserts that were only sweet. I used to gorge myself on sugary enchantments: British supermarket sweets such as flapjacks; boxes of syrup-drenched gulab jamun; trays of sticky Turkish baklava; plates of cinnamon-scented Portuguese pastéis de nata . . . But while I do still enjoy these treats, I've learnt how to adjust them to my adult palate – either by adding a flavour twist or by consuming them with something that balances out their sweetness (such as black tea or coffee). I suppose I never fell out of love with sweetness, per se, I just fell in love with the other tastes: sour, salty, bitter, umami. Which is why incorporating these flavour profiles into desserts makes them all the more delicious – not just for me, but for everyone.

Our palates naturally change as we transition from kid to teenager to adult. There's a reason the likes of Haribo, Starburst, Skittles and Fruitella are geared towards children: they're predominantly sweet, and fairly limited in flavour. As we age, most of us seem to leave this sweet obsession behind and gain greater appreciation for bitter flavours such as dark chocolate, coffee and booze. This is not about 'sophistication': biology has a lot to do with it. As children, our senses are extremely, well, sensitive: we respond more strongly to light, colour, texture and taste because the aim of the game is to survive, and sugar cravings feed into this. Anyone with kids (or who has babysat them) will know that giving them free reign of the cookie jar will lead to an annoyingly hyperactive evening. Kids don't have an 'off' button when it comes to sugar, because sugar is a high-energy food that delivers maximum calories, thereby supporting the goal, which is growth. Once we've reached adulthood, pursuing calories isn't as urgent.

Other significant changes take place over the course of our adult lives. Our taste buds die: the average person starts with 10,000 of them, but eventually they stop regenerating and our sense of smell dulls – another reason that we seek stronger flavours as we get older. We also build a deeper and broader library of experiences and memories – meals shared with those we love, holidays spent languorously enjoying local food, new tastes experienced with new friends. So much of our enjoyment of food is contextual. As stated by sensory psychologist Marcia Pelchat, 'Liking bitter melon or hoppy beer isn't about bitterness sensitivity. It's about exposure, motivation, interest. It's all cultural.' More foods are fair game in adulthood because we no longer crave only the one-note sweetness that punctuated our childhoods. We are more taken with food experiences that deliver on multiple taste and sensory levels – that are sweet and sour and salty, hot and cold, crunchy and smooth. Our brains love the stimulation, and this understanding is at the heart of how I think about desserts.

on flavour

taste versus flavour

'Taste' and 'flavour' are often used interchangeably and, mostly, that's fine. But given this is part of a series of cookbooks on taste, it's important to clarify how they are different: taste is a component of flavour, while flavour is the whole picture.

Taste refers solely to the bitter/sour/salty/sweet/umami qualities of an ingredient – i.e. what our taste buds, the mushroom-like receptors on our tongues, can distinguish. So, if we were to suck on a lemon, and then eat a passionfruit, our tongue would recognise both ingredients as sour, but it would not be able to distinguish between the lemon and the passionfruit – even though we know that they are not the same.

Enter flavour. Flavour is not just what the taste buds pick up on the tongue, but also what the olfactory system (our sense of smell) registers in the nose. The distinctions between different ingredients – and what we often mean when we talk about their flavour – are largely determined by aroma. Hundreds of volatile chemicals contribute to aroma, in thousands of combinations. The result? Endless flavour possibilities. But with so many options, it becomes hard to develop a useful vocabulary. The five tastes, on the other hand, are contained, and easier to grasp, so they form a good foundation for understanding flavour.

Finally, there is your palate: your individual ability to distinguish between and appreciate different flavours. Part of what determines our sensitivity to the different flavour profiles (sweet, salty, sour, bitter, umami) are the genes we inherit, which code our specific set of taste buds. Some of us are supertasters with more taste buds than the average person and a greater sensitivity to different tastes; some are 'taste blind' and relatively insensitive to stronger flavours. But exposure, life experiences and memories also play an important part in how we register flavour. So, getting to understand how taste and flavour work in general, but also what your palate prefers, is essential.

taste + flavour intensity

A general principle to bear in mind is that the combination of two different tastes (e.g. sweet and sour) is likely to result in something that registers as less intense on the tongue than if they were consumed individually, because they offset each other.

A natural example of this is a piece of fruit: an extremely underripe, sour peach has very little sugar (the sugar is stored as tasteless starch) and will cause your mouth to pucker up with the intensity of it. Equally, a mushy, overripe peach will have such a high sugar content that you might find it overwhelmingly sweet. A perfectly ripe peach, however, has both acidity and sweetness in balance so that you get the very best expression of that fruit's flavour: because no single taste dominates, you're fully able to absorb and experience all the aroma compounds that convey the wonders of that peach. What's going on in that single piece of fruit is representative of what we want to achieve in our cooking. Making delicious food is, in part, about balancing the different tastes to create a flavour profile that is both exciting and harmonious.

understanding your palate

It would be neat to be able to give you a set of precise rules for how to combine tastes and flavours – but life is rarely that simple. Each of us is different, and so the way that we experience taste and flavour can vary, too. We do not all have the same sensitivities – what is hugely sweet for one person may not be very sweet for someone else; likewise with bitterness, sourness, saltiness and umami. This is something to be celebrated,

because it means that there is no right or wrong: there is only what *you* like.

Getting to understand your own palate (as well as your family's and friends') will ultimately empower you to make subtle adjustments when cooking that result in something that is delicious to you (and whoever you're cooking for).

As an example: I tend towards sour and bitter, whereas my friend Jade veers towards sweet. So, when I shake us up a cocktail, I might add a little more lemon to mine and a little more sugar syrup to Jade's – these subtle adjustments ensure that I get my ideal cocktail and she gets hers.

Understanding your palate also makes it a lot easier to work out what cuisines you might appreciate most and what to order at restaurants – it's a form of getting to know yourself better.

---

recipes to play with

---

double coconut granola (page 115)

sweeter Consider stirring dried mango or pineapple into your granola once baked.

less sweet Swap the coconut oil with a grassy, subtly bitter extra virgin olive oil for a more savoury backnote. Or try the chocolate version for something a little more bitter.

---

brown butter brown sugar brownies (page 45)

sweeter Opt for a higher proportion of milk chocolate and/or some sweet mix-ins such as marshmallows or white chocolate chips.

less sweet Use only dark chocolate, add a touch of ground cardamom and/or top with cocoa nibs. If umami is your thing, incorporate 3 tablespoons of white miso into the batter.

---

white chocolate, miso + sesame cookies (page 144)

sweeter Leave out the miso and swap the sesame seeds for chopped pecans.

less sweet To lean more into the umami/funky flavours swap the white chocolate with caramelised white chocolate (e.g. Valrhona's Dulcey) – or you can make your own

the function of sugar

Sugar is one of the building blocks of food and comes in many forms. It's one of the first things we experience on this earth: we get lactose from our mother's milk (or formula) and it's our very life blood in those first few weeks and months. So while sugar has been villainised for its role in the global obesity and diabetes epidemics, it's also true that, without it, there would be no life on earth. And without sugar there would also be less pleasure and flavour all round.

You and I both know that sugar sweetens, but it does many other things in our cooking, including:

Sticking food together
(e.g. flapjacks, croquembouche)

Preserving fruits and vegetables by drawing out the moisture that would otherwise breed bacteria (jams, marmalades, chutneys, pickles)

Stabilising foods like meringues and mousses

Thickening and adding body or bulk (syrups, glazes, wine)

Retaining moisture in baked goods

Inhibiting gluten and ice structures, meaning more tender cakes and smoother ice creams

Creating glossy glazes

Seasoning food
(most processed foods – even savoury ones – contain sugar)

Promoting caramelisation, a process of browning that contributes to colour and flavour (a world without roasted flavours would be a miserable one)

Feeding fermentation
(wine, kombucha, bread)

Providing decoration
(sculptural sugar work, etc.)

Creating rise in bakes (creaming butter and sugar together is a mechanical form of leavening, whereby the sugar crystals cut through the fat, trapping air bubbles in the batter)

Sugar can do ALL these things because it's 'hygroscopic': it likes, attracts and holds water. Said another way: sugar and water are in a long-term, highly co-dependent, sometimes unstable relationship. Both like to be around each other a lot – they subscribe to the 'two becomes one' relationship philosophy – but sugar is particularly clingy, regularly dissolving into water at any opportunity.

types of sugar

Let's take it back to GCSE Science for a second to better understand the different ways that sugar appears in this world. Sugars can be categorised in multiple ways and at various levels:

1   chemical (at a molecular level)

2   botanical (which plants produce which sugars)

3   mechanical (how sugars are processed)

4   commercial (what we see on the supermarket shelves)

1   chemical

At a chemical level, sugar represents the building blocks that combine to create various substances. There are lots of different types of sugar molecules ('saccharides'), including glucose, fructose, sucrose, maltose and lactose. All of these have different compositions and come from different sources:

monosaccharides

a single sugar molecule

examples:
glucose
fructose

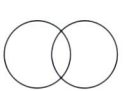

disaccharides

2 sugar molecules

examples:
sucrose (glucose + fructose)
lactose (glucose + galactose)

oligosaccharides + polysaccharides

more than 3 sugar molecules
(polysaccharides = 10+)

examples:
cellulose
starch

syrups

more than 1 sugar molecule,
suspended in water

examples:
honey
maple syrup

2   botanical

Sucrose is the main sugar we encounter day to day – it's those white grains we're all familiar with. Of the world's sucrose, 80% comes from sugar cane, which grows in tropical climates such as Brazil and India, and the other 20% comes from sugar beet, which grows in temperate climates such as Europe. We produce refined and unrefined sugars from sugar cane, but only refined sugars from sugar beet.

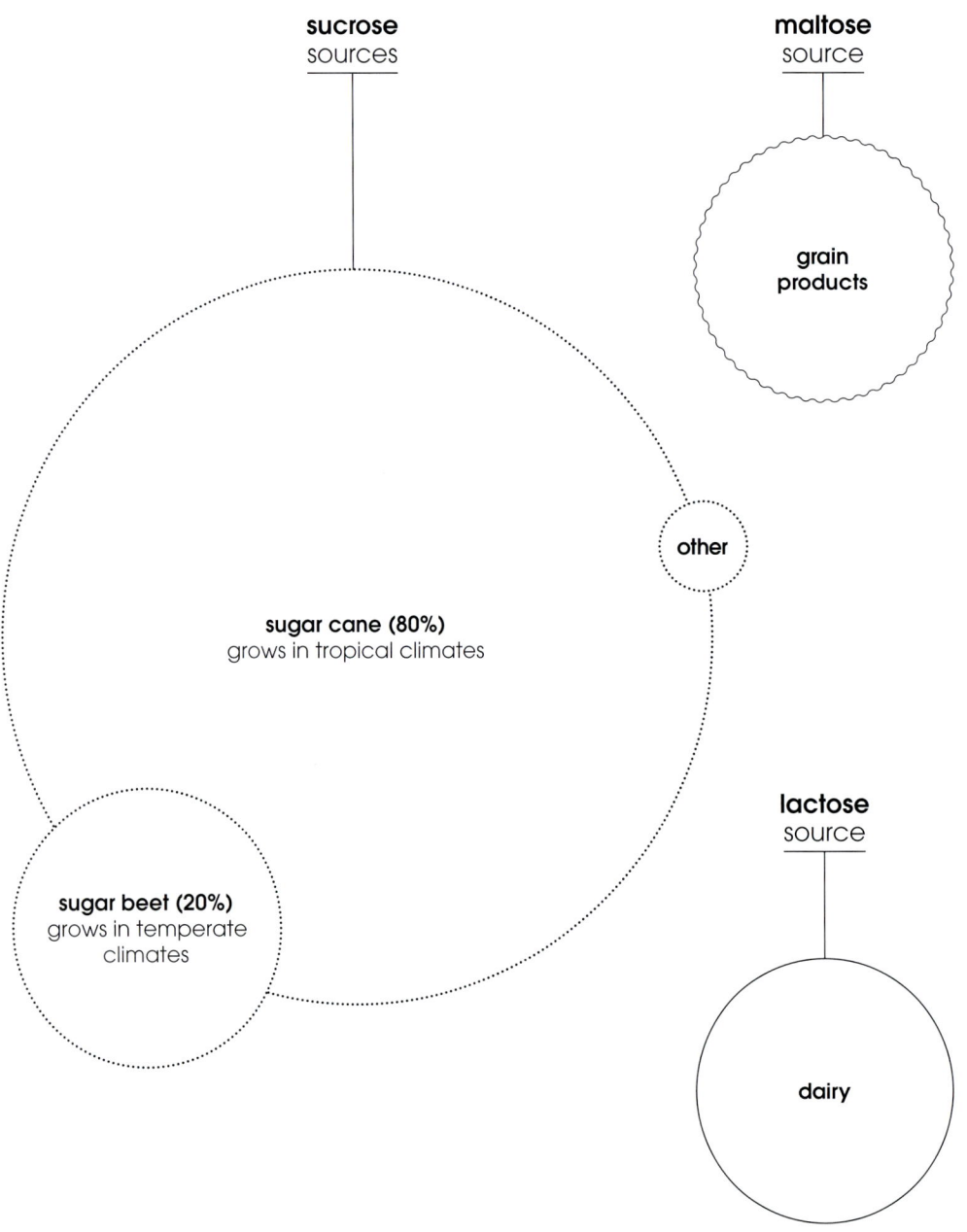

sucrose
sources

maltose
source

**grain
products**

other

sugar cane (80%)
grows in tropical climates

lactose
source

sugar beet (20%)
grows in temperate
climates

dairy

3   mechanical

All white sugar is refined, whereas brown sugar can be refined (e.g. soft light brown sugar), partially refined or unrefined (e.g. light muscovado), more of which in the Brown Sugar chapter (page 35).

4   commercial

The refined and unrefined sugars produced from sugar cane and sugar beet make their way onto the supermarket shelves in different forms – either as dry crystals (which we tend to categorise according to size, e.g. granulated vs caster/superfine sugar) or as syrups (molasses, treacle, golden syrup, etc.). There are also syrups derived from other sources such as honey (which comes from the flower nectar collected and processed by honeybees) and maple syrup (made from the sap that comes from the sugar maple tree).

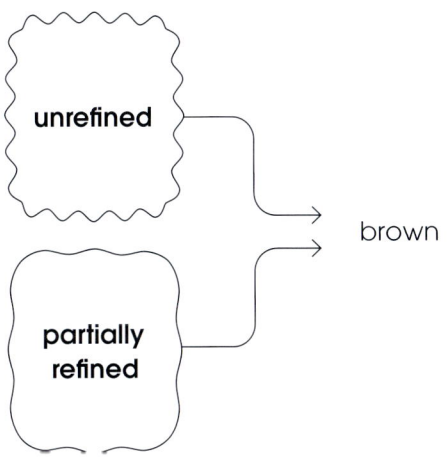

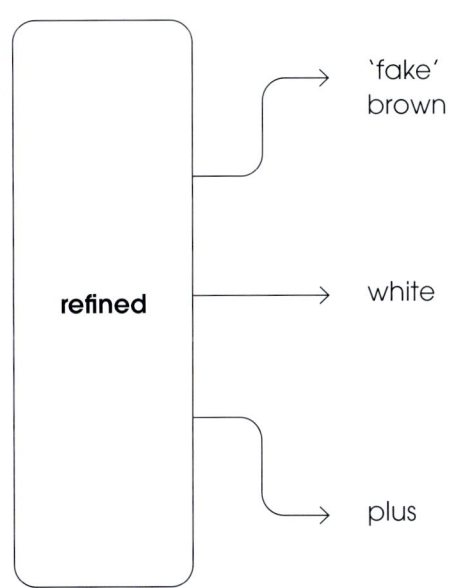

○	maple syrup
⬡	honey
◖	jaggery
⬭	palm sugar
⏢	panela
○	muscovado
◇	demerara

△	soft light brown
△	soft dark brown

⬚	icing (confectioners')
⬚	caster (superfine)
◇◇	granulated

⬡	cubed
⬡	pearled

unlocking knockout desserts

Unlocking knockout desserts is about finding the sweet spot between harmony (comfort) and contrast (interest). And, for this, you have three fighters:

1   flavour

2   texture

3   temperature

flavour

Early in my cooking journey, by the side of Miss P (my former boss from my fishmongering days and the very best home cook I know!), I learnt about Thai cuisine. While making tom yum gai soup, Miss P explained rot chad – a concept central to Thai cuisine – which approximately translates to 'the right taste': that all dishes are fundamentally a balance between salt, sourness, heat and sweetness, with one or two typically taking the leading roles (rot chad naam, 'primary taste') and the rest being supportive (rot chad rong, 'secondary taste'). It's a concept not only applied at the level of an individual dish, but also to the structure of a meal.

I first learnt of rot chad when I was a novice cook, but immediately latched on to it as a framework, because I realised that the five tastes (sour, salty, sweet, bitter and umami) could be thought of in the same way – as a series of elements to balance and choose from to create both harmony and contrast in a dish. It's an approach that has informed my cooking ever since. I use it to identify if something is missing, or when I'm deciding what to cook for friends and want to create a feast that will suit their palates.

Samin Nosrat's *Salt, Fat, Acid, Heat* discusses the popularity of salted caramel, explaining that its wide appeal lies in the fact that it hits all the taste notes (salty, sour, bitter, umami *and* sweet). This makes sense when you consider that the more tastes there are present in a food, the more of your taste buds are activated (and the greater the variety of aromas, too). All of this adds up to maximum flavour impact.

My rot chad-inspired framework – which is essentially all about balancing flavours – is helpful regardless of what you're cooking, but it particularly comes into its own with desserts.

We might reasonably expect to experience sourness, saltiness, bitterness and umami in savoury food, but they're not such an obvious choice for desserts. Don't get me wrong: they are often present, just mostly acting undercover. Collectively, we probably don't realise that one of the reasons so many of us love chocolate or coffee or lemon in our desserts and bakes is because they are an antidote to sweetness.

When you're putting together a dessert, sweetness is a given, but you also need to consider which elements are offering some contrast. Is it sour berries (see page 141)? Dark chocolate (page 179)? Umami-rich miso (page 144)? Savoury sesame seeds (page 58)? Bitter-edged booze (page 104)? Acidic molasses (page 48)? Zingy lemon (page 159)? This is the key to desserts that will make people go back for seconds.

texture + temperature

To understand how texture and temperature can enhance our food, it's helpful to understand what is known as 'the ice cream effect'. Ice cream is inherently exciting to our palates because it gives us temperature and texture changes in one mouthful: the ice cream goes from frozen to melted on the heat of our tongue. As this happens, the texture changes from solid and slightly chewy to smooth and liquid. This encapsulates the concept of dynamic contrast: the moment-to-moment contrasts we experience from foods whose properties are changing as we eat them. Dynamic contrast typically increases how palatable foods are to us.

Texture is a deeply personal aspect of food, thus hard to make sweeping generalisations about. Still, in a restaurant setting, chefs think actively about contrasts in textures: for example, the snap of pastry against the pillowy softness of cream against the toothsome quality of berries. Contrasts in texture equal greater sensations, which makes a dish more interesting to eat. Well-considered textural contrasts can elevate a dish, and this is as true in home cooking as in professional kitchens. Many familiar dishes illustrate this:

Smooth soups garnished with crunchy croutons

Buttery guacamole scooped up with crisp tortilla chips

Tapping through the brittle caramelised crust of a crème brûlée to the silky cream below

Thick, unctuous cheesecake cream atop a sandy, malty biscuit base

It's not about learning to make cheffy dishes like Michelin-starred Massimo Bottura's 'Five Ages and Textures of Parmesan' (a dish using a single ingredient presented in five different textures:

a soufflé, a sauce, a mousse, a foam and a wafer), it's about keeping texture in mind as you cook.

Part of the success of a knockout tiramisu lies in soaking the sponge fingers just the right amount. Not enough, and the coffee isn't soaked all the way through, meaning their dry texture and bland flavour interrupts the eating experience. Too much, and they melt soggily into the cream, leaving everything just a bit *too* soft. Sometimes elevating a luscious, smooth chocolate mousse is as simple as a scattering of nubbly cocoa nibs and a drizzle of silky extra-virgin olive oil. Sometimes, we are not looking for extremes: sometimes the aim of the game is to be all soft, full stop. No hard and fast rules, but something to simply bear in mind as you cook and create in the kitchen.

Temperature contrasts, meanwhile, offer a sensation that straddles confusion and excitement. It's a tool that sits less comfortably in savoury cooking, but works well in desserts, as sugar gets very hot while there are several dessert elements designed to be eaten very cold (ice cream, sorbets, etc.). Cooler-climate countries often deliver fantastic desserts because they can lean into warm and hot puddings, and then contrast that with something cool or cold. In the realm of desserts and puddings, the meeting of two temperature experiences in one mouthful is an exciting one!

examples to try

hot 'n' cold berries with white chocolate + cardamom (page 141)

peach melba galette (page 102)

blackened bananas with coconut, passionfruit + ginger (page 67)

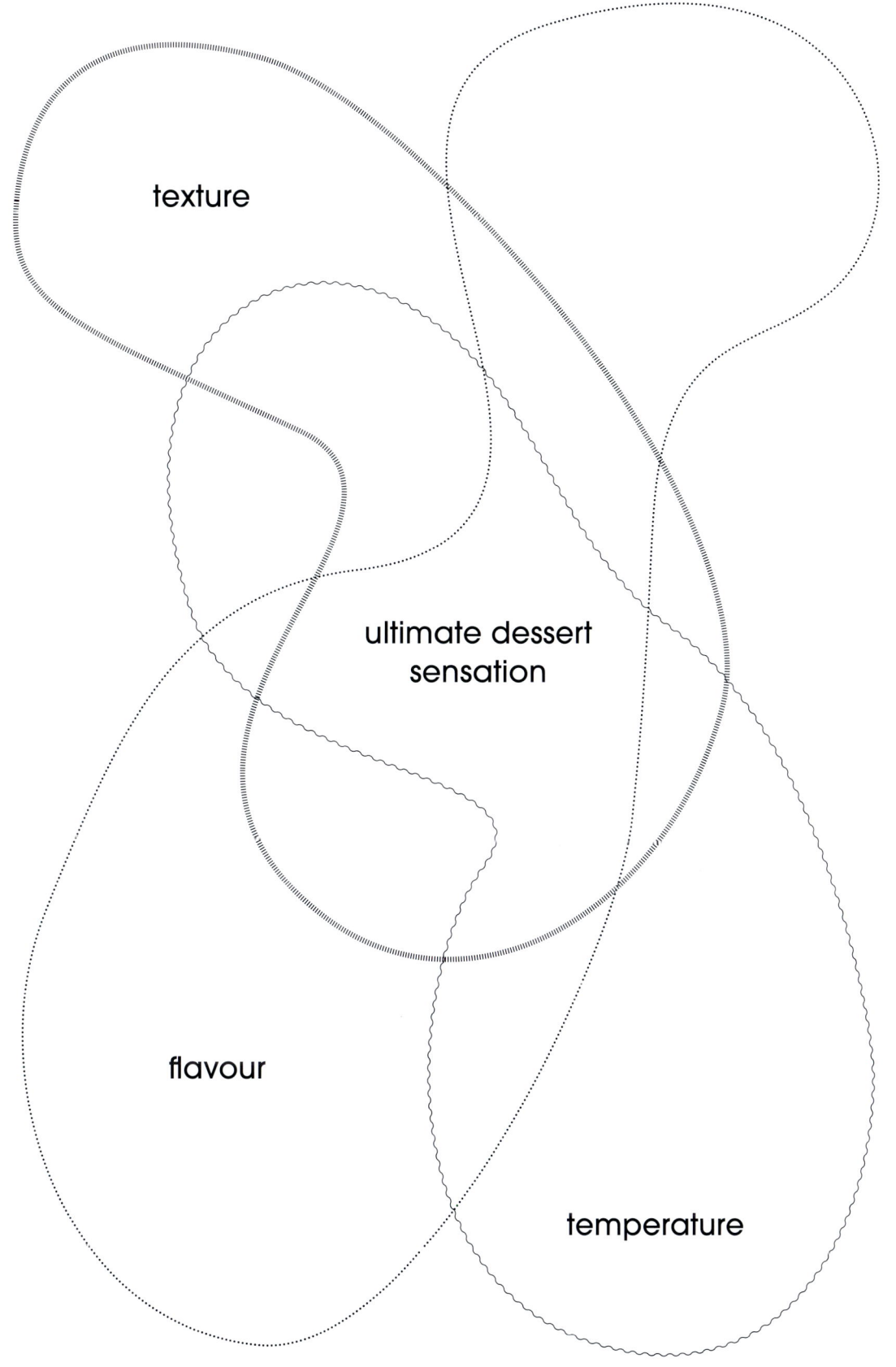

texture

ultimate dessert
sensation

flavour

temperature

how to build
knockout desserts

		ice cream	set custard
Start with your base	The base you opt for will dictate what you layer over the top in terms of flavour, temperature and texture contrast	OOOO○○○○	OOOO○○○○
1 balance the flavours	**Add extra sweetness** to low sweetness bases. Or alternatively, employ more flavour contrast to bring any added sweetness into balance.	maybe	maybe
	Add **flavour contrast** – particularly if you have a highly sweet base, or you've incorporated additional sweet ingredients.	maybe	✓
2 add temperature contrast	For example taking very cold ice cream and pairing it with something hot, or warming up a cake and pairing it with cold cream.	✓	maybe
3 overlay texture contrast	Something hard or crunchy will typically always benefit from something soft and/or creamy, but this is not necessarily the case the other way around (completely soft desserts can be very nice).	✓	maybe

	sweetness level
OOOO OOOO	sweetness level
(temperature bar)	temperature level
∿∿∿∿	texture level

	biscuit	meringue	dough	cake	pastry	batter
sweetness	OOOOOO OO	OOOOOOOO	O OOOOOOO	OOOOO OOO	OOO OOOOO	OO OOOOOO
temperature	(half yellow)	(half yellow)	(half yellow)	(half yellow)	(half yellow)	(full orange)
texture	∿∿∿∿∿∿∿	∿∿∿∿∿∿	∿∿∿∿	∿∿∿	∿∿∿∿∿	∿∿∿
	✗	✗	✓	maybe	✓	✓
	✓	✓	maybe	maybe	✓	maybe
	maybe	✗	N/A	✓	maybe	maybe
	maybe	✓	maybe	maybe	✓	maybe

the great british pud

I have a deep appreciation for the elegance of desserts: a wobbly, melt-in-the-mouth panna cotta, a towering soufflé, a crisp tarte fine aux pommes . . . but, truly, nothing beats a Great British pud.

Outside of the UK, 'pudding' typically denotes a type of custard-based dessert thickened with cornflour, not dissimilar to Angel Delight. It is a single species of dessert, and the only thing that changes about it is the flavour – vanilla, banana, chocolate, butterscotch, strawberry, etc. But in the UK the term 'pudding' goes beyond this: it's commonly used to cover a particular brand of dessert that is comforting and homely. As an example, a soufflé would always be described as a dessert, while an apple crumble would be described as pudding.

British cuisine is typically laughed out of the (gastronomic) room, but the thing is: we know what makes a good end to a meal. I guarantee you no other cuisine – okay, apart from French – has such an extensive and strong roster of after-dinner treats. Part of the reason for the strength of British desserts – which I believe is also a factor in the weakness of our savoury dishes – is our cold climate. British food at its best is simple, steadying and satisfying; at its worst, heavy, stodgy and bland. Stodginess is not a particularly desirable quality in savoury foods, where the inclusion of meat can make for a very heavy experience, but it can be quite welcome in desserts, where a degree of stodginess delivers ultimate comfort. Our cold winter nights also demand *warmth*, which is why most British puddings are served that way. So while a sticky toffee pudding will never have the finesse of a French tarte Tatin, I know which one I would rather curl up with in front of the fire on a winter's day, after a long walk. Let's face it: we Brits have never been all that good at elegance, but boy, do we nail cosy – and this is what our puddings deliver.

texture contrast | plush cake
nubbly walnuts
silky cream

temperature contrast warm sponge
hot sauce
cold cream

flavour balance | sweet dried figs
caramel-like butterscotch
tangy crème fraîche
subtly bitter walnuts

5 tips to elevate your baking

---

1 don't be afraid of salt

---

2 make the most of seasonal fruits
Nothing else delivers as much flavour.

---

3 bake when you have time and are feeling calm
Don't rush key processes like creaming together butter and sugar until light and fluffy, or giving your pastry plenty of opportunity to rest, or kneading that dough until the gluten is fully developed.

---

4 the fridge is your best friend
Pastry and biscuit doughs like to be chilled down before they're baked and, once cooked, many desserts are improved by an overnight rest in the fridge (brownies and chocolate tortes, cheesecakes, etc.)

---

5 demerara (or turbinado) sugar is the baking ingredient that gives you the most bang for your buck
The crackly crust it gives cakes and scones makes them considerably more delicious, and also prettier.

cook's notes

salt

Flaky sea salt has twice the volume of fine sea salt, so where a recipe asks for 1 teaspoon of flaky sea salt, you could substitute this with ½ teaspoon of fine sea salt (and vice versa).

Not all salts are equally salty – I use Maldon for my flaky sea salt, and supermarket own-brand fine sea salt. I tend not to use iodised salt as I find it has a chemical flavour.

eggs + dairy

Eggs are UK medium or large (i.e. whatever I have in the house) unless specified.

I strongly recommend using full-fat dairy throughout. Fat content does make a difference to the final result.

Butter is slightly salted, unless otherwise specified.

baking

Flour is plain flour, unless otherwise specified.

Sugar means either white caster or white granulated sugar, unless otherwise specified.

1 teaspoon vanilla bean paste can be repaced with ½–1 vanilla pod instead. I generally do not recommend using vanilla essence or extract, although there are some exceptions (e.g. in cakes).

Gelatine leaves are platinum grade.

time

Time is a key ingredient in the kitchen for two reasons:

1. it can allow flavours to deepen and harmonise;

2. it allows proteins (e.g. in eggs, gluten, etc.) to relax, which ultimately results in better texture.

It's rare that a recommendation to, for example, rest a cheesecake overnight, is essential to a recipe working; but in following through you will be rewarded with a superior result for little extra effort.

recipe list

for breakfast

banana + sesame soufflé pancakes **58**

peachy cornbread pancakes **98**

laura's coconut-filled pancakes (sri lankan pani pol) **112**

jamaican cornmeal porridge **114**

double coconut granola **115**

rice porridge with rhubarb + vanilla **135**

berber 'nutella' (moroccan amlou) **157**

breakfast croissant pudding with anise pears **175**

currant dutch baby with honeyed ricotta **192**

iranian fried eggs with dates **216**

for comfort

apples + blackberries with brown sugar breadcrumbs **44**

salted molasses fudge **48**

crêpes with plantain + rum caramel **68**

banana, chocolate + tahini brioche pudding **69**

rice pudding soufflé cake with sumac strawberries **93**

coconut cream pie with passionfruit **118**

little vanilla bean pots with plums **138**

vanilla apricots with a hot sugar crust **140**

blackcurrant, bay + clotted cream cake **163**

fierce ginger, pear + pepper cake **178**

black tea eccles cakes **196**

hot buttered apples with bay custard **202**

sticky figgy pudding with walnut butterscotch **204**

for speed

terrazzo cookies (chocolate, caramel, pistachio) **40**

brown butter brown sugar brownies **45**

toasted anzac biscuits **124**

vegan coconut + lime loaf **125**

simple citrus, olive oil + vanilla loaf **142**

white chocolate, miso + sesame cookies **144**

raspberries + sour cream **154**

little lemon + honey cakes **159**

french yoghurt pot loaf **160**

chocolate + pear self-saucing pudding **179**

cranberry welsh cakes **193**

far breton **194**

apple mincemeat filo pie (pastis gascon) **197**

for dinner parties

for weekends + celebrations

for summer lunches + picnics

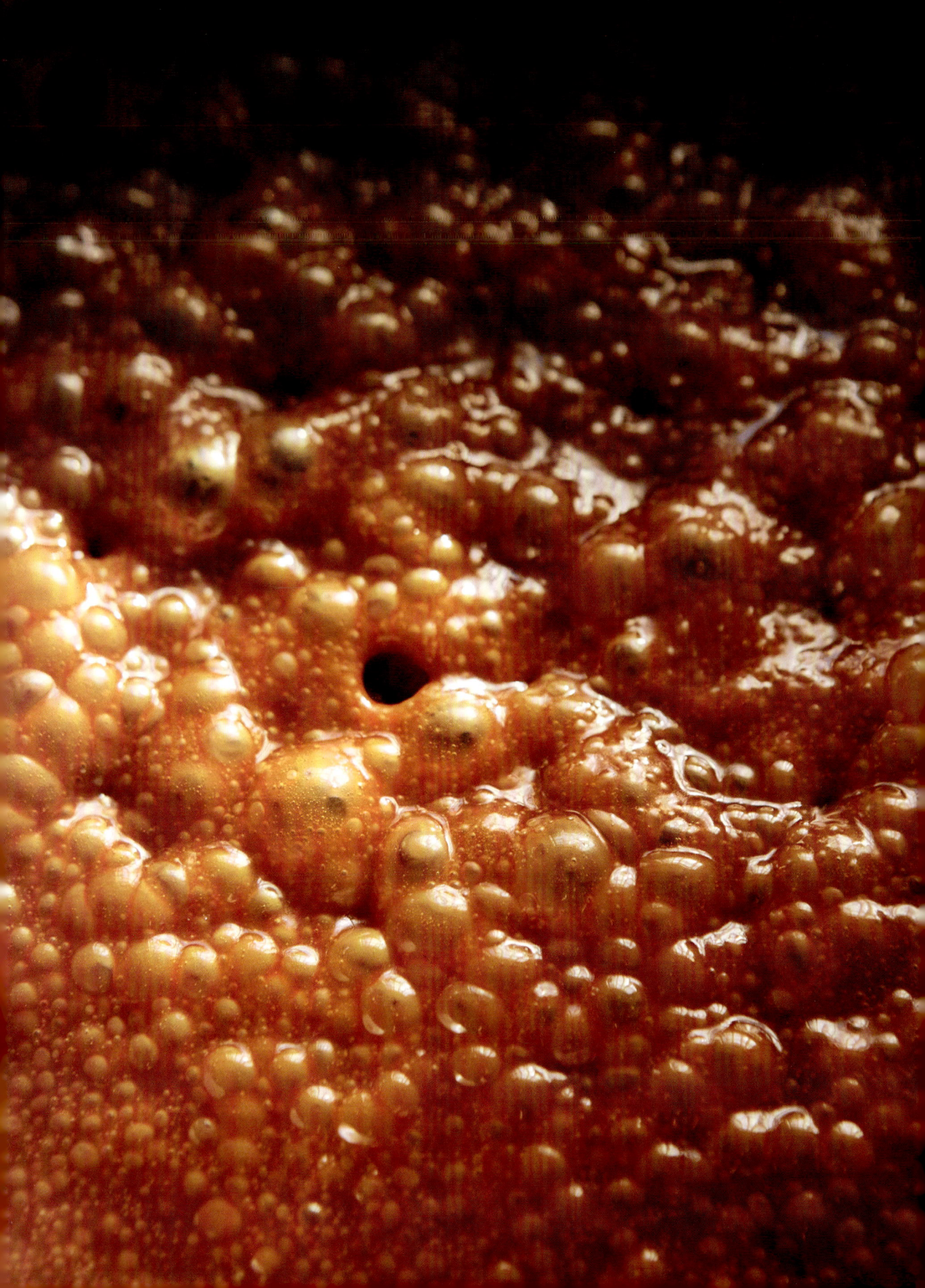

brown sugar

black sugar crème caramel **39**

terrazzo cookies (chocolate, caramel, pistachio) **40**

carrot halwa cake **42**

apples + blackberries with brown sugar breadcrumbs **44**

brown butter brown sugar brownies **45**

rum + grapefruit babas **46**

salted molasses fudge **48**

cardamom brioche loaf **50**

Colourless, odourless and neutral: refined white sugar is a staple in most baking cupboards because it is predictable, unchanging, convenient. White sugar will deliver a fine-crumbed, light sponge; it'll help your cakes glow golden; and it will do all of this in the background, never asserting itself onto the flavour of your bakes. No one could argue that white sugar isn't useful, but there is a trade-off, and that trade-off is personality. White sugar might be eminently functional, but brown sugar brings the (metaphorical) spice and can offer a new dimension to your desserts.

White versus brown is an age-old battle that has been waged across continents, cultures and industries – and the business of sugar is no exception. The process of producing white sugar is one of extracting sucrose from sugar cane (or beet), leaving behind thick brown molasses. Meanwhile unrefined (or partially refined) brown sugars have a proportion of the molasses left in them. In the nineteenth century, US company Domino Sugar – a white-owned business with limited control over black sugar production – mounted a smear campaign against brown sugar, circulating microscopic photographs of the harmless but visually off-putting microbes that live in brown sugar. Accordingly, people flocked to buy the white stuff and cooking authorities such as Mrs Lincoln in her 1897 *Boston Cook Book* extolled its virtues: 'all brown sugar and moist sugars are inferior in quality . . . loaf (white) sugar is purest.'

But today – especially against a backdrop of greater concerns around health – unrefined sugar is sexy again. These days we might actively highlight the use of muscovado in a baked good or molasses in a cookie: these are desirable descriptors that indicate less processing and greater depth of flavour. But this change of heart has certainly resulted in more complex manufacturing processes. Have you ever wondered about the difference between light brown sugar and light muscovado, or treacle and molasses? They seem the same – they function the same – but they are produced differently: the former are refined versions of the latter. For example, dark muscovado is an unrefined brown sugar (which naturally contains molasses); whereas dark brown sugar is refined white sugar that has had the molasses that was previously removed added back in to resemble . . . dark muscovado. Circuitous? Frustratingly so. And it's a familiar story; the preference for ultra-refined, 'pure' white versions of staples such as bread, flour or rice has frequently seen raw ingredients put through intensive processing, only for these to end up in knots once it becomes clear that the 'brown' versions have their own merit.

It is counterintuitive, but the darker the sugar, the less sweet it becomes – not because brown sugar has materially less sucrose (it's around 95% vs caster/superfine sugar's 99%) but because it contains things that white sugar doesn't: fructose, glucose, amino acids, minerals. The result is sugars that have a degree of acidity, bitterness and earthiness. Thick, sticky molasses is the most extreme example at only 50% sucrose – try it by itself and it'll make your mouth pucker, but this acidity is an asset when it comes to balancing out sweetness (see the Salted Molasses Fudge on page 48). It's also a quality that bicarbonate of soda (baking soda) can play off in baked goods to help them rise.

But let's get down to practical stuff. The varieties of white sugar available in the supermarket (caster/superfine, granulated, icing/confectioners' sugar) vary in texture rather than flavour – icing sugar being the finest, granulated the coarsest. With brown sugar, however, there's a whole world of flavour: from the subtle caramel tones of golden caster sugar through to viscous, bittersweet treacle. While light brown sugar and light muscovado (etc.) are interchangeable, I prefer the unrefined versions for their more nuanced flavour. This won't make a difference in all recipes but it can be key to elevating desserts where brown sugar is the star, for example in set custards and creams. Meanwhile, demerara sugar – those glassy, caramel-tinged granules – is wonderful for the texture and sparkly finish that it adds to more rustic bakes.

Beyond the brown sugars typically found in the supermarket, there are others: jaggery from India and Southeast Asia, panela/rapadura and piloncillo from Central and Latin America, Okinawa black sugar from Japan. What most have in common is that they have been reduced until solid in form and intense in flavour, ranging from smoky (piloncillo) to toffee-ish (jaggery) to liquorice-like (Okinawa black sugar). Using jaggery in the Carrot Halwa Cake (page 42) therefore feels organic, while the use of black sugar in the Crème Caramel (page 39) delivers nuanced flavour for something with so few ingredients. Derivatives of brown sugar exist too, such as Caribbean browning – a caramel made with brown sugar that is added to stews for depth of flavour and to black cake, the Caribbean version of a Christmas cake (page 203).

The merits of brown sugar are many: flavour (those earthy, caramel-y, even smoky notes), quicker caramelisation and moisture (from the hygroscopic nature of molasses, see page 17). But perhaps, at the end of the day, all you need to do is listen to D'Angelo's 1995 neo-soul classic *Brown Sugar*: the song wouldn't have been half as sexy had white sugar been the metaphor.

black
sugar
crème
caramel

This recipe calls for Okinawa black sugar, which has a unique complexity of flavour and can be purchased online. Alternatively, sub it for dark muscovado.

The crème caramels will need at least 24 hours (but ideally 48 hours) in the fridge to allow the eggs to settle and the caramel to soak into the custard properly, ensuring a neat turnout.

balancing elements
Okinawa black sugar
(subtly sour, subtly salty)
dark caramel (bitter, sweet)

Baking and pastry are generally more formula-based than savoury cooking, which allows the geek among us (hello, it's me) to get excited about things like ratios. All of this to say that in this recipe I've done the maths for you: I wanted to understand the perfect balance of whole eggs to yolks in a crème caramel, and I think this is it. Beyond formulas, there is flavour: in this case dark, salty, malty Okinawa black sugar provides a depth that takes the humble crème caramel to new heights.

Makes 6 deep or 8 shallower crème caramels

100g (3½oz/½ cup) Okinawa black sugar
500ml (17fl oz/generous 2 cups) whole milk
½ tsp vanilla bean paste
¼ tsp fine sea salt
2 eggs
3 egg yolks

for the caramel
130g (4½oz/generous ½ cup) caster (superfine) sugar
130ml (4½fl oz/generous ½ cup) water

equipment
6–8 dariole moulds, about 200ml (7fl oz) capacity – or similar
deep baking dish large enough to accommodate all the moulds

1 Preheat the oven to 150°C fan/170°C/340°F/gas 3. Briefly blend the Okinawa black sugar until there are no lumps. Rinse out your dariole moulds with water and place by the stove.

2 In a saucepan, bring the sugar and water for the caramel to a gentle simmer over a medium heat (swirl the pan from time to time but do not stir). Turn the heat up to medium-high and wait for it to start to turn golden – this can take up to 15 minutes, but big bubbles will appear on the surface when the time is nearing. From this point, turn the heat down again and watch it like a hawk. Remember: you control the heat, so you are the boss of the caramel! Take the caramel to a mid (verging on dark) amber, then remove it from the heat and swirl the pan to allow the residual heat to take it a little further. Take the caramel as far as you can without burning it, then immediately pour it into the moulds and swirl it up the sides (move quickly as the moulds will get hot and the caramel will set in seconds – washing up gloves are useful to protect your hands!).

3 For the crème, heat the milk, half of the Okinawa sugar, vanilla and salt gently in a pan until warmed through. Meanwhile, put a full kettle on to boil.

4 In a jug or bowl, gently stir together 1 whole egg with the remaining Okinawa sugar until there are no lumps (try not to incorporate much air into the mix). Next, stir in the remaining egg and yolks until incorporated. Mix in the warm milk, then strain the mixture through a sieve into your moulds (leaving 1cm/½ in at the top). Cover each with foil.

5 Place the ramekins in a deep baking dish and pour in boiling water from the kettle to reach halfway up the sides. The dish you use to hold the crème caramels will significantly affect how quickly they bake – a metal tray will take around 15–20 minutes, while a ceramic dish may take double that, so check accordingly. You're looking for the caramels to be set but still with a wobble in the middle. Carefully remove the moulds from the water and remove the foil. Set aside to cool before chilling in the fridge overnight – or, for best results, 48 hours.

6 To serve, run the tip of a fine knife around the edge of each crème caramel, just a millimetre or two, to help release the edges. Dip the bottom 3mm/⅛in of each mould in freshly boiled water for 10–15 seconds to help melt the caramel, then invert onto a plate and, holding the mould against the plate, give it a firm shake to release. If it's not coming out, dip the mould deeper into the hot water and repeat.

terrazzo cookies (chocolate, caramel, pistachio)

This dough requires several hours in the fridge, or overnight.

You can also pop these in the freezer, ready to slice (do take care) and bake whenever the mood takes you.

You could replace the chocolate, caramel and pistachios with your favourite chocolate or nuts, etc.

balancing elements
dark chocolate (bitter)
dark caramel (bitter)

These are a shortbread cookie masquerading as an Italian tile, and I'm a little obsessed. The caramel shards folded through the cookies (along with dark chocolate and pistachios) add a fun texture, but the inclusions are really up to you – she's a flexible cookie.

Makes around 24

200g (7oz) unsalted butter, softened
100g (3½oz/½ cup) caster (superfine) sugar
½ tsp vanilla bean paste (or extract)
300g (10½oz/scant 2½ cups) plain (all-purpose) flour
½ tsp fine sea salt
40g (1½oz) dark chocolate, coarsely chopped
50g (2oz/⅓ cup) shelled pistachios, coarsely chopped

for the caramel shards
100g (3½oz/½ cup) granulated (or caster/superfine) sugar

for the sugar coating
1 egg white, lightly whisked
50g (2oz/¼ cup) demerara (turbinado) sugar

equipment
electric hand mixer
silicone baking mat (e.g. Silpat) or greaseproof paper

1   Make the caramel shards by melting the sugar in a frying pan until you have a deep amber caramel (since this is a dry caramel, you *are* allowed to stir this as it melts). Pour onto a silicone mat (or some greaseproof paper), then spread it out quickly using an offset spatula (or back of spoon). Leave to cool completely, then use the end of a rolling pin to gently bash up the caramel until you have a rubble of shards – none should be larger than 5mm (¼in).

2   In a large bowl, beat together the butter, sugar and vanilla until pale and fluffy, around 2–3 minutes with an electric whisk. Add the flour and salt, and mix until just combined – no longer (don't worry if the mixture still appears a bit crumbly). Stir through the caramel shards, chocolate and pistachios.

3   Divide the dough in half and tip the first half out onto a sheet of cling film (plastic wrap). Shape into a log about 4–5cm (1¾–2in) in diameter – this might not be easy, on account of all the additions to the dough, but persevere! Wrap tightly in the cling film. Repeat with the second half of the dough. Chill both logs in the fridge for at least 3 hours, or overnight.

4   When ready to bake, preheat the oven to 160°C fan/180°C/350°F/ gas 4 and line two large baking trays with silicone baking mats or greaseproof paper. (If you don't have two large baking trays, you can simply cook the biscuits in two batches.)

5   Unwrap the dough logs, use a pastry brush to coat in the egg white, then roll them in the demerara sugar until evenly coated. Cut each log into rounds about 1.5cm (¾in) thick and place on the baking trays, well spaced. Bake until the edges are firm and starting to turn golden but the middles still look light, around 15–20 minutes. Remove from the oven and leave to cool completely before serving.

Tip Any biscuit or cookie dough, as well as pastry, hugely benefits from an overnight rest in the fridge. It ensures that the flour is properly hydrated and that the gluten has had a chance to relax. What this means for you is dough that is easier to work with and gives a better result when baked (less spread, more height).
See also: White Chocolate, Miso + Sesame Cookies (page 144).

carrot halwa cake

Leave the eggs (along with the butter and cream cheese) out of the fridge in advance of baking, as it is essential to them whipping up sufficiently.

If using butter instead of ghee when making the halwa, keep a closer eye on it as it is more liable to burn.

Was the crossing of Indian carrot halwa with American carrot cake inevitable? I think so. Here the two are combined to create a restrained single-layer cake with fragrance and richness of flavour coming from the beautifully spiced carrot halwa base. And there is perhaps no more perfect recipe for this book, given that halwa comes from the Arabic word hulw, meaning 'sweet'.

balancing elements
cardamom (bitter)
ginger (hot, bitter)
turmeric (bitter)
cream cheese (sour/tangy)

Serves 8–10

for the halwa
60g (2¼oz) ghee (or butter)
50ml (2fl oz/3 tbsp plus 1 tsp) neutral oil (e.g. sunflower)
1 tsp ground cardamom
½ tsp ground ginger
¼ tsp ground turmeric
generous grating of fresh nutmeg
¾ tsp fine sea salt
around 300g (10½oz) carrots, peeled or scrubbed and coarsely grated
1 x 170g (6oz) tin of evaporated milk

for the cake
2 eggs, at room temperature
70g (2¾oz/⅓ cup) caster (superfine) or granulated sugar
70g (2¾oz/¼ cup) light muscovado (or light brown) sugar
½ tsp baking powder
¼ tsp bicarbonate of soda (baking soda)
170g (6oz/1¼ cups plus 1 tbsp) plain (all-purpose) flour
40g (1½oz/generous ¼ cup) sultanas (golden raisins)

for the icing
75g (3oz) butter, softened
40g (1½oz/2½ tbsp) powdered jaggery (or light muscovado sugar)
1 tbsp honey
¼ tsp ground cardamom
1 x 165g (5½oz) pack of full-fat cream cheese, at room temperature
1–2 tbsp pistachio slivers, to garnish

equipment
20cm (8in) non-stick, loose-bottomed cake tin, with sides at least 5cm (2in) tall
electric hand whisk or stand mixer

1   Preheat the oven to 160°C fan/180°C/350°F/gas 4 and line the base of your cake tin with greaseproof paper.

2   Melt the ghee in a large saucepan over a medium heat, then pour 3 tablespoons out into a separate jug or bowl (leaving 1 tablespoon in the saucepan). Add the oil to the ghee in the jug and set aside.

3   Returning to the saucepan, add the spices and ½ teaspoon of the salt to the ghee and allow to bloom for 1 minute before stirring through the grated carrot. Cook for 10 minutes, stirring every so often until the carrot has softened. Add the evaporated milk and simmer gently for 5 minutes, then take off the heat and set aside.

4   Meanwhile, make the cake batter. Use an electric whisk or stand mixer to whisk together the eggs, sugars, baking powder, bicarb and remaining ¼ teaspoon of salt until the mixture reaches ribbon stage, around 3–5 minutes. Scrape the bowl down with a spatula halfway through.

5   If the ghee mixture has solidified, reheat it gently. Continuing to whisk, slowly stream the ghee mixture into the batter. Sift in half of the flour and fold through gently until partly incorporated. Fold through half of the halwa, again just until partly incorporated. Repeat with the remaining flour and halwa, then fold in the sultanas until fully combined.

6   Pour the batter into the prepared tin and bake until golden brown, springy in texture and a skewer comes out clean, about 30–40 minutes. Allow to cool fully before icing.

7   To make the icing, use an electric hand whisk to beat together the butter, jaggery (or light muscovado), honey and cardamom until light and smooth (if your honey is in a solid state, gently warm it before using). Loosen the cream cheese by giving it a brief whisk or stir (I do this with a small whisk directly in the pack), then add to the butter mix and fold together until combined. (If you've used jaggery and the icing feels a bit loose, the addition of 1–2 teaspoons of cornflour/cornstarch should help.)

8   To serve, use a serrated bread knife to slice off the slight dome on the top (chef's treat) and then turn it upside down so that you have a completely flat surface. Spread over the cream cheese icing then sprinkle the pistachios on top.

Tip If your dried fruit has been in the cupboard a while and is a bit dry, you can plump it back up by soaking in a couple of tablespoons of boiling water (or hot rum/brandy).

apples +
blackberries
with brown sugar
breadcrumbs

Wild blackberries are particularly wonderful here because of their tartness, but supermarket varieties also work.

Best served with cold cream or ice cream.

To make this gluten free, swap the bread for a gluten-free option. To make it vegan, swap the butter for plant butter.

balancing elements
Bramley apples (sour)
wild blackberries (sour)
sourdough (subtly sour)
light muscovado (subtle acidity)

There is no question that my death-row dessert would be my late grandmother's apple and blackberry crumble, but do we need another recipe for crumble? I'm going to say no. Instead, here's a classic British flavour combination that has taken a road trip across the United States: this is what Americans call a 'brown betty', a combination of stewed fruit topped with sweetened breadcrumbs. It's a bit more 'everyday' than crumble, and a great use of day-old bread. Texturally, the breadcrumb topping, which is toasted in butter and brown sugar, gives a satisfying spongy-chewy-crunchy texture that is delicious against the softness of the cooked apples. And if you use a good sourdough loaf for the breadcrumbs you also get a slight tang from the topping, which plays beautifully against the sweet-tart Bramley cooking apples and blackberries: heaven!

Serves 4–6

juice of 1 lemon
3 Bramley apples
3 Pink Lady apples
3 tbsp caster (superfine)
   or granulated sugar
¼ tsp fine sea salt
100g (3½oz) blackberries

for the brown sugar breadcrumbs
90g (3¼oz) butter
75g (3oz/¼ cup plus 1 tbsp)
   light muscovado
   (or light brown) sugar
¼ tsp fine sea salt
180g (6oz/3 cups) fresh breadcrumbs
   (I like sourdough)

equipment
23cm (9in) round pie dish
   (or similar)

1 Preheat the oven to 170°C fan/190°C/375°F/gas 5.

2 Add the lemon juice to your pie dish, then prep the apples: peel, cut into quarters, remove the cores and cut each quarter into six roughly square pieces. Add these to the pie dish as you go, periodically tossing the apples in the lemon juice to prevent them from browning. Once all the apples have been prepared, stir through the sugar and salt.

3 Bake for 40 minutes, giving the apples a stir halfway through (don't worry if some of the apples break down to mush – this is what we want!).

4 Meanwhile, make the topping. Melt the butter in a frying pan (skillet), then stir through the sugar and salt until dissolved. Take off the heat and stir through the breadcrumbs.

5 Remove the apples from the oven and turn it up to 180°C fan/200°C/400°F/gas 6. Stir the apples to help them break down further, add in the blackberries, then top with the breadcrumbs. Bake until the top is golden and crispy in parts, around 20 minutes. Allow to cool for 15 minutes before serving.

Tip Different apple varieties not only have different flavours but also behave differently when subjected to heat. In dishes like this, as well as apple crumble and apple pie, I like to combine cooking apples (which are sharp and break down completely when cooked) with a variety such as Pink Lady (which is sweet and keeps its shape when cooked). This achieves a contrast in flavours and textures.

butter brown sugar brownies

I've specified a mix of dark chocolate and milk chocolate with a high cocoa content (sometimes also called 'semi-sweet' – I use Guittard). If you can't easily get hold of this, opt for a mix of 220g (8oz) dark chocolate and 80g (3oz) standard milk chocolate.

I highly recommend Meunier cooking chocolate when baking.

I also love the shape, texture and flavour of these brownies when baked in silicone financiers moulds (which yields around 20 individual brownie fingers) – however, bear in mind that they will take considerably less time to bake.

balancing elements
dark chocolate (bitter)
brown butter (subtle umami)
light muscovado (subtle acidity)
salt

Brownies can be the very best or the very worst – and, like cheesecake, there is a wide range in people's preferences. Some like 'em cakey, some fudgy; some extremely dark, some milk-chocolate-heavy; some embellished, some kept pure . . . This recipe is my idea of the perfect brownie: dark, fudgy and unadorned. There are no spices or swirls, but toasty browned butter and caramel-like brown sugar work as sultry backnotes to the chocolate. In other words: deep, dark bliss.

Makes 16 brownie squares

160g (5½oz) salted butter, plus (optional) extra for greasing
100g (3½oz) dark chocolate (at least 70% cocoa solids), roughly chopped
100g (3½oz) milk chocolate (at least 45% cocoa solids), roughly chopped
4 eggs
120g (4oz/½ cup) caster (superfine) sugar
120g (4oz/½ cup) light muscovado (or light brown) sugar
80g (3oz/⅔ cup) plain (all-purpose) flour
25g (1oz/2 tbsp plus 1 tsp) cocoa powder
¼ tsp fine sea salt
flaky sea salt, to garnish

equipment
20cm (8in) square non-stick baking tin
electric hand whisk

1 Preheat the oven to 160°C fan/180°C/350°F/gas 4. Line your tin with greaseproof paper.

2 Place the chocolate in a heatproof mixing bowl. Separately, in a small metal saucepan (so you can see it change colour), melt the butter over a low heat. Once melted, turn the heat up to medium and allow the butter to simmer gently until it turns golden and smells nutty, up to 10 minutes. At this point, keep an eye on it constantly and take it to a deep golden brown, removing it from the heat as soon as it's reached this level (as it will continue cooking beyond this moment). Allow to cool for 5 minutes, then pour the browned butter (milk solids and all) straight over the chocolate. Leave to sit for 2 minutes before stirring until the chocolate is completely (or mostly) melted.

3 In a large bowl, use an electric whisk to mix the eggs and both sugars just until evenly combined. Gently fold in the melted chocolate and butter, then sift in the flour and cocoa powder, and add the salt. Fold the flour gently into the mix, stopping as soon as everything is combined – you should be left with a glossy batter.

4 Pour the brownie mix into the prepared tin. Sprinkle with some flaky sea salt, then bake for around 35–40 minutes until the top is glossy and an inserted skewer comes out with damp crumbs (you want to err on the side of undercooked with brownies). Eat warm or leave the brownies to cool in their tin (they will cut more neatly if allowed to fully cool and set). They're at their best the next day.

Tip Allowing chocolate tortes and brownies to rest overnight makes them even more delicious – it gives the eggs time to settle, which improves the texture, and gives all the complex flavours of chocolate time to meld.

rum + grapefruit babas

It's important that your yeast is the active dry kind (rather than fast action).

Use the best rum that you can buy – I like Mount Gay Black Barrel, or a spiced rum would also be lovely here.

balancing elements
grapefruit (sour, bitter)
dark rum (subtly bitter)

There is something figuratively (and literally) intoxicating about a dessert that almost knocks you out with booze. And while rum babas aren't particularly cool, I like to think of them as the French grandfather of desserts – one that you might come to appreciate in later years. The grapefruit does a lot here, bringing a floral quality that works beautifully against the rum.

Makes 12–14

for the sponge
50ml (2fl oz/3 tbsp plus 1 tsp)
    whole milk
5g (¼oz/1¾ tsp) active dry yeast
50g (2oz/⅓ cup) strong white
    bread flour

for the babas
75g (3oz) butter
3 eggs
1 tbsp runny honey
zest of ¼ grapefruit, plus
    extra to serve
125g (4½oz/1 cup) strong
    white bread flour
pinch of fine sea salt

for the syrup
400g (14oz/2 cups) caster (superfine)
    or granulated sugar
200ml (7fl oz/generous ¾ cup) water
200ml (7fl oz/generous ¾ cup) high-
    quality rum, plus extra to serve
3 strips of grapefruit peel
juice of 1 grapefruit
    (around 60ml/2½fl oz/¼ cup)

for the Chantilly cream
200ml (7fl oz/generous ¾ cup)
    double (heavy) cream,
    fridge-cold
1 tbsp icing (confectioners') sugar
1 tsp vanilla bean paste

equipment
12-hole non-stick cupcake tin,
    greased well
piping bag (helpful, not essential)
temperature probe
    (helpful, not essential)

1   For the sponge, heat the milk in a pan to 30°C (85°F) (or until just warm to the touch – this will take mere seconds). Whisk in the yeast and flour. Leave to sit at room temperature for around 30 minutes. At the same time, melt the 75g of butter in a small saucepan, then leave to cool slightly.

2   Whisk together the eggs, honey and grapefruit zest in a bowl, then incorporate the sponge. Add the flour a spoonful at a time, whisking well to get the lumps out. Finally, whisk in the melted butter and salt until you have a glossy batter of dropping consistency. Pipe or spoon the batter into the prepared cupcake tin until the holes are half full, then prove for around 30 minutes until risen and roughly doubled in size (see tip).

3   Preheat the oven to 170°C fan/190°C/375°F/gas 5.

4   Bake the babas until they are golden and firm to the touch, about 10–12 minutes. Leave to cool for a couple of minutes, then turn out and place on a wire rack.

5   Meanwhile, make the syrup by combining the sugar, water, rum and grapefruit peel in a medium saucepan. Bring to the boil and simmer until syrupy and reasonably viscose, around 7–10 minutes. Remove the peel, stir in the grapefruit juice and set aside to cool down slightly.

6   When the babas are still slightly warm, soak them in the syrup for up to 1 minute, flipping a few times, until they are moist but still holding together. Strain any crumbs out of the syrup and reserve for serving.

7   To serve, whip up the cream, icing sugar and vanilla until soft peaks form. Separately, brush the babas lightly with some neat rum. Plate the babas in shallow bowls and add a couple of tablespoons of syrup to each to create little moats around them. Top with a spoonful of cream (or pipe it on for extra wow factor), then grate over a little grapefruit zest.

Tip To create a reliable environment to prove dough, turn your oven on for exactly 60 seconds, then turn it off – this will create a perfectly warm environment. See also: Cardamom Brioche Loaf (page 50) and Bee Sting Cake (page 164).

salted molasses fudge

This requires a few hours to set and dry out (the more it dries out, the better it gets).

Molasses is my preference, but you could also use treacle here.

balancing elements
molasses (sour, subtly bitter)
salt

Fudge is the pure embodiment of sugar, and not for the faint of heart. I loved it as a kid and my obsession is still going strong. This fudge is intense, with the molasses lending a slightly bitter-umami taste (not dissimilar to coffee) that ups the ante from a flavour perspective but avoids a sickly-sweet aftertaste.

Fudge can be smooth, creamy and slightly chewy (Cornish clotted cream fudge), or sandy and crumbly (Scottish tablet). I'm personally with the Scots on this one, and this recipe reflects that.

Makes around 50 squares

70g (3oz) butter
500g (1lb 2oz/2½ cups) caster (superfine) sugar
140ml (5fl oz/generous ½ cup) whole milk
200ml (7fl oz/generous ¾ cup) condensed milk
70g (3oz/3 tbsp) blackstrap molasses
½ tsp flaky sea salt, plus extra for sprinkling

equipment
20cm (8in) square cake tin (or similar)
temperature probe/sugar thermometer
electric hand mixer (optional)

1   Line your tin with 2 long sheets of parchment paper, letting the excess overhang the tin edges to act as a sling when removing the fudge later.

2   Melt the butter in a large, heavy-based saucepan over a medium-low heat. Stir in the sugar and milk, then cook until the sugar has dissolved, around 2–3 minutes. Turn the heat up to medium and bring the mixture to a light simmer, allowing it to bubble away for 5–8 minutes.

3   Add the condensed milk, molasses and flaky sea salt. Stir to combine, then bring to a simmer and allow to gently bubble away for 15 minutes. At the 12-minute point, start regularly checking the temperature – you want it to hit 115°C (240°F). As soon as it does, remove the pan from the heat and beat with an electric hand mixer until the mixture starts to thicken, around 3–4 minutes (this will take longer if beating by hand).

4   Pour the mixture into the prepared tin and sprinkle with extra flaky sea salt. After 20 minutes, deeply score squares into the mixture with a knife. Allow to set for several hours (or ideally overnight) before breaking into squares.

cardamom brioche loaf

This recipe takes a few hours from start to finish (with a decent proportion of this time being hands off), so it makes a good weekend project!

This makes two loaves (for all the effort, you may as well), but any brioche that you don't eat on the day can be sliced and frozen, perfect for toasting or epic French toast.

You can make the whole recipe through in a single day or split it over two.

It's important that your yeast is the active dry kind (rather than fast action).

balancing elements
cardamom (bitter)
yeast/fermentation (umami)

I don't really understand the obsession with cinnamon buns. The dough is rich and sweet, cinnamon is rich and sweet, and the icing they're often topped with? Rich and sweet. But a light, billowy loaf of brioche with cardamom bun energy? Yes, please. Cardamom, with its subtle bitterness and complex flavours of resin and menthol, works beautifully here, cutting through the sweet caramel notes of the brown sugar and ensuring that, once baked, it's never long for this world.

Makes 2 loaves

120ml (4fl oz/½ cup) whole milk
6g (¼oz) active dry yeast
80g (3oz/generous ⅓ cup) caster (superfine) or granulated sugar
170g (6oz) butter, softened, plus extra for greasing
260g (10oz/2 cups plus 1 tbsp) strong white bread flour
6 eggs, at room temperature
1½ tsp fine sea salt
260g (10oz/2 cups plus 1 tbsp) plain (all-purpose) flour

for the cardamom sugar coating
140g (4¾oz) butter, melted
140g (4¾oz/¾ cup) light muscovado (or light brown) sugar
7 tsp (around 14g) ground cardamom

equipment
temperature probe (helpful, not essential)
2 x 900g (2lb) loaf tins
stand mixer

1   Heat the milk in a pan to 35°C (95°F) or just warm to the touch – this will take mere seconds. If splitting the process over two days, drop this temperature down to 30°C (85°F). Add the milk to the bowl of your stand mixer, along with the yeast and a teaspoon of caster sugar. Cover and leave to sit for 10 minutes – after this point the yeast should be activated and bubbly. Meanwhile, grease your tins with butter (if you only have one tin, you may have to bake the loaves one at a time).

2   Add the rest of the sugar, strong bread flour, eggs and salt to the milk mixture, and mix until combined. Next, add the plain flour until combined. Continue to mix the dough, scraping the bowl down from time to time, until it becomes less sticky, starts to pull away from the side of the bowl and becomes shinier and more elastic. This will take 10–13 minutes.

3   With the mixer running, add the butter a tablespoon at a time, allowing it to be fully incorporated before adding more – it will take you a good 10–12 minutes to incorporate all the butter. Proceed to mix the dough for a further 5 minutes until it passes the windowpane test (you should be able to pull the dough quite thin, so you can see the light through it – like a window – without it tearing easily/immediately, see the photograph on page 52). Cover the bowl and let it rest until doubled in size, around 1–1½ hours (see tip, opposite).

4   Punch down the dough so that it's deflated. If making over two days, this is the point at which to cover with cling film (plastic wrap) and place in the fridge overnight – otherwise continue on.

5   Turn the dough out onto a lightly floured surface and split it in half. Divide each piece into 5 pieces, roughly even in size. Use your hands to flatten each piece of dough into a rectangle, then perform a 'letter fold' by folding a third of the dough down into the centre, then folding the remaining dough at the bottom over the top (it can be helpful to look at a diagram or video online before doing this). Turn the piece 90 degrees, then flatten it out as much as you can, before pulling 1cm (½in) or so at the top of the dough down and pinching it tightly, then rolling the dough towards you into a log shape, as tightly as possible (see photo overleaf). Set aside on a baking tray lined with greaseproof paper.

6   Now prepare your cardamom sugar coating station. Add the melted butter to a shallow bowl. Combine the brown sugar and ground cardamom on a small plate or tray. One by one, dip the rolled pieces of dough into the melted butter (or you could brush it on), then add to the tray of sugar and gently cover the rolled pieces with sugar using your hands. Ensure each piece is fully coated, then place inside the prepared tins until they're all tucked in alongside each other (there should be 5 pieces in each tin).

7   Cover the tins with cling film and leave to prove in a warm place until doubled in size, around 1–1½ hours (see tip).

8   If you have been proving your dough in the oven, remove it now, then preheat the oven to 190°C fan/210°C/410°F/gas 6.

9   Bake the loaves in the oven, turning the heat down to 170°C fan/190°C/ 375°F/gas 5 after the first 10 minutes, until a deep golden brown – around 30 minutes in total. (If you have a temperature probe, the internal temperature should register around 90–95°C/195–200°F). Allow to cool for 5–10 minutes, then tip the loaves out of their tins. Serve while still warm.

Tip To create a reliable environment to prove dough, turn your oven on for exactly 60 seconds, then turn it off – this will create a perfectly warm environment. See also: Rum + Grapefruit Babas (page 46), Bee Sting Cake (page 164) and Rosemary Milk Buns (page 212).

bananas + plantain

banana + sesame soufflé pancakes **58**

roasted banana butterscotch budino **60**

jamaican hummingbird cake **62**

blackened bananas with coconut, passionfruit + ginger **67**

crêpes with plantain + rum caramel **68**

banana, chocolate + tahini brioche pudding **69**

banoffee coffee sundae **70**

The humble banana: nature's shrink-wrapped, portable, perennial snack. Walmart's bestselling product. Fairtrade symbol. Stalwart of our fruit bowl. Why is this fruit so popular worldwide? And why hasn't its cousin, plantain – a staple in countries across Southeast Asia, Africa, the Caribbean and Latin America – ever hit the mainstream in the 'West'?

Bananas surround us. Not only present on the shelves of every supermarket, they feature throughout mainstream pop culture: from comedy staple (the banana peel slip of Vaudeville theatre), to art (Andy Warhol's design for Velvet Underground's debut album), to language ('the crowd went bananas', etc.), to music (Gwen Stefani's noughties pop classic 'Hollaback Girl'). All this might lead you to perceive it as a jovial, occasionally absurd symbol (no doubt helped by its phallic shape). Or worse, boring: in every supermarket, fruit bowl and packed lunch (each of us eats an average of 130 bananas per year according to the United Nations). But the history books tell us otherwise: bananas and politics go (corrupt) hand in (corrupt) hand.

Bananas were first cultivated in Southeast Asia but reached the Americas in the 1500s, marking the beginning of an industry that would come to sit at the centre of twentieth-century Central American history – a history of wars, coups, corruption and communism. And at the centre of the banana industry? The United Fruit Company (UFC), a corporation as ubiquitous in the twentieth century as Google is today, and which came to be known as *el pulpo* ('the octopus') for all the tentacles it had in lots of different places (and pockets).

Sam Zemurray – who would come to run UFC and be known as the 'Banana King' – arrived in America as an uneducated, penniless Russian-Jewish immigrant. In part, then, the story of bananas is a story of how an entrepreneurial and hard-working individual achieved 'the American Dream'. But it's also very much about the dark side of American capitalism. UFC came to have such a stranglehold on Latin American politics that it became hard to distinguish where the company ended and the US government began. I don't have the space to detail this mad tale, but Rich Cohen's *The Fish That Ate the Whale* is a worthwhile read. It'll have you echoing Gwen Stefani: 'This shit is BANANAS.'

Although many kinds of bananas exist – big, tiny, yellow, red, with seeds and without – most of us eat the exact same fruit. Have you noticed that bananas don't vary in flavour (only in ripeness)? Commercial bananas have been cultivated to be sterile, so each banana is a clone of the last. This lack of biological diversity makes bananas both a supremely viable export crop and a risky one. Today, the banana variety exported *en masse* is the Cavendish but it used to be the Gros Michel, which was not only sweeter but also easier to slip on. The Gros Michel dominated global markets until it was wiped out by a single infection in 1910 – which might explain why we don't see people slipping on banana skins anymore.

Today, the Cavendish remains core to our eating habits: it makes a great snack, is the star ingredient in banana bread and a perfect partner to caramel, nuts, cinnamon and chocolate. However, this may not last. As Dan Koeppel[1] warns: '(Every) banana scientist I spoke to . . . says it's not an "if", it's a "when" . . . It only takes a single clump of contaminated dirt . . . to get (an infection) rampaging across entire continents.' Conclusion: don't let their ubiquity make you complacent about enjoying them – the Cavendish may not be forever.

Plantain (said plant-TIN, I won't hear otherwise), meanwhile, does not share the banana's ubiquity in the West, but it is a staple in the cuisines of the Caribbean, Central and South America, Africa and southern India. Thought to have originated in New Guinea several thousand years BC, it later spread along trade routes to Indo-China and East Africa. African slaves taken to the Caribbean prepared plantain as they would have at home, which explains the similarities between the cooking of plantain in the Caribbean and West Africa today. In short, the story of plantain is the story of migrants.

While we tend to eat bananas raw, plantains are cooked because of their high starch content. Underripe green plantain is grouped with yam and potatoes as 'ground provisions', such is its heavy, dry, rubbery quality; but as it ripens it changes significantly: the starchiness drops, the texture softens, and its sweetness comes out – which lends plantain an addictive quality for both savoury and sweet dishes. Andi Oliver said it best: 'There's a certain beauty to a sweet thing that lives in a savoury world.' And that's how I felt as a child, eating fried plantain straight out of the frying pan at my grandmother's house.

---

1 Author of *Banana: The Fate of the Fruit that Changed the World*

banana + sesame soufflé pancakes

Best suited to a treat breakfast for two, rather than brunch with friends, as these are a little more involved than your average pancake.

There is no added sugar in this batter (because: bananas, Nutella, maple syrup), but you could add some, if you have a particularly sweet tooth.

balancing elements
white sesame seeds (subtly bitter)
black sesame seeds (subtle umami)

I am a pancake person through and through. Which is to say: pancakes > waffles, Pancake Day > Valentine's Day and pancakes > a fry up. And as you might expect from such a statement, I've tried most types of pancakes. Crêpes will always have a special place in my heart given a childhood spent in France, and I love the ease of whipping up a stack of American pancakes, but when you want something a little special you can do worse than turning to the Japanese for some guidance.

The Japanese have elevated many things, and the humble pancake is no exception. By separating the eggs, whipping up the whites and then folding these through the batter, Japanese pancakes (which these are inspired by) have this lighter, more ethereal texture. Typically, Japanese pancakes are elegantly plain, but in a distinctly un-Japanese move I've added banana to the batter (for sweetness), a sesame-seed crust to the outside (for savouriness) and an optional melting chocolate middle (hello, Nutella). I regret nothing.

Makes around 6

3 ripe bananas
½ tsp fine sea salt
½ tsp ground cinnamon
1 tsp vanilla bean paste
3 eggs, separated
5 tbsp self-raising flour
cooking spray or butter, for cooking
2 tbsp each white and black sesame seeds, combined
6 tsp Nutella (optional)
maple syrup, to serve

equipment
pastry rings, 8cm (3in) in diameter (or similar), 3cm (1in) high
large frying pan (skillet) with a lid

1 Roughly mash the banana with the salt (I like there to still be a few chunks of banana left), then add the cinnamon, vanilla and egg yolks. Fold through the flour.

2 Whisk the egg whites to stiff peaks, then gently fold through the banana mixure.

3 Grease the pastry rings with butter. Heat a frying pan over a medium heat, then spray with cooking spray (or add ½ tablespoon of butter allowing it to melt and start foaming – if using butter, you might need to turn down the heat if it seems like the butter is getting too toasty). Add the pastry rings to the pan (you may have to cook the pancakes in two batches), then add 1–2 teaspoons of the sesame seeds into the rings so that the base is covered by a thin layer. Spoon in the pancake batter until the base is covered, then add a teaspoon of Nutella to the centre. Cover the Nutella with more batter until it sits around 7mm (¼in) below the top of the ring. Add a splash of water to the pan and cover with a lid for around 5–7 minutes.

4 Slide a spatula underneath the rings and swiftly flip them over. Cook with the lid off until they've puffed up further and spring back when touched, around 1–2 minutes. Remove from the pan and run a spatula or thin knife around the edge to help loosen the sides. Lift the rings off, either with a pair of tongs or with your hands (they will be hot, so use a tea towel to protect your fingers). If you're cooking the pancakes in two batches, scrape any sesame seeds out of the pan before cooking the next batch.

5 To serve, create a stack using 2–3 pancakes, then douse in maple syrup and eat immediately.

roasted banana butterscotch budino

These require a stint in the fridge to set.

This will make more caramel sauce than you need (making a smaller quantity doesn't really work) – store leftovers in the fridge for up to 5 days and drizzle over ice cream.

Nice served with crème fraîche and a little biscuit or biscotti.

balancing elements
caramel (bitter/sweet)
dark rum (subtly bitter)
dark muscovado (acidic)
salt

Budino is simply the Italian word for pudding (the Angel Delight kind), but it sounds much sexier so we like it better (hello, marketing). And while pudding is typically a childish, cosy kind of dessert, this is not that: this is a properly adult re-imagining of that school dinners classic, banana custard. Adapted from a recipe by pastry chef Dahlia Narvaez, the deep, rum-spiked butterscotch base of these little desserts, combined with caramelised banana, is guaranteed to seduce.

Makes 6–8

1 banana
90g (3¼oz/½ cup) dark muscovado (or soft dark brown) sugar
60ml (2½fl oz/¼ cup) water
1 tsp vanilla bean paste
½ tsp flaky sea salt
200ml (7fl oz/generous ¾ cup) double (heavy) cream
270ml (9fl oz/generous 1 cup) whole milk
1 egg
2 egg yolks
2 tbsp cornflour (cornstarch)
1 tsp dark rum (optional)
1 tbsp unsalted butter
crème fraîche, to serve

for the caramel sauce
120g (4½oz/½ cup plus 2 tbsp) caster (superfine) sugar
2 tbsp butter
120ml (4fl oz/½ cup) double (heavy) cream
¼ tsp flaky sea salt

equipment
6–8 x 90ml (3fl oz) glasses (or ramekins/espresso cups)
temperature probe (helpful, not essential)

1 Preheat the oven to 240°C fan/260°C/500°F/gas 10. Lightly prick the banana all over with a small knife, then place on a lined baking tray and roast for 20 minutes, until blackened and soft. Set aside to cool before splitting the skin and scooping out the cooked banana flesh.

2 Stir together the dark muscovado sugar, water, vanilla and salt in a small saucepan and bring to a simmer over a medium-high heat. Cook, regularly swirling the pan, for 10 minutes until it has started to become more viscose. Whisk in the mashed banana and cook for another 2 minutes. Whisk in the cream and milk, then allow to heat back up, around 4–5 minutes.

3 In a separate bowl, whisk together the egg, yolks and cornflour until there are no lumps. Whisk a quarter of the caramel mixture into the eggs, followed by the rest, using a spatula to make sure the pan is left clean. Strain the egg mixture back into the pan, turn the heat down slightly to medium, then whisk continuously until smooth and thick like classic Bird's custard. This should take around 10 minutes (if you have a temperature probe, you're looking for it to get to around 80°C/175°F). Remove from the heat, whisk in the rum and butter, then divide among the serving glasses, filling each around two-thirds full. Allow to cool, then place in the fridge to set for around 1 hour.

4 Make the caramel sauce by cooking the sugar over a medium heat until it has fully melted and you have a fluid, clear, amber caramel. Whisk in the butter, followed by the cream and the salt. Allow to cool, then pour over the puddings and put them back in the fridge to set for another 3 hours or so. To serve, top each with a teaspoonful of crème fraîche with a little biscuit alongside, if liked.

jamaican hummingbird cake

The cakes can be made a day or two in advance and wrapped tightly with cling film (plastic wrap). The icing can be made a day in advance – just re-whip when ready to use (and loosen with a little milk, if needed).

Do use Philadelphia cream cheese for the icing, to ensure it has the right consistency and stability.

Dried pineapple flowers can be purchased online, or alternatively you can make them yourself by following a recipe online.

My sandwich cake tins are 5cm (2in) tall – if yours are shorter, try splitting the batter across three tins (you may have to bake them in two batches, and they won't take as long to bake).

balancing elements
cream cheese (sour/tangy)
ginger (hot, subtly bitter)

Hummingbird cake is carrot cake's exuberant cousin, with a little banana bread energy thrown in for good measure. If you like either of those two classics, you'll like this just as much. It's a warmly spiced cake, moist from bananas and pineapple, and topped with the sweet-salty tang of cream cheese frosting.

The hummingbird is the national bird of Jamaica, and the cake's name is thought to have stemmed from its being sweet enough to attract them. As one of a handful of recipes that the Jamaican Tourism Board distributed to America with a view to enticing more visitors to the island, it's a true testament to the power of food. Today, this cake is well loved in the southern states of America – it's been Southern Living*'s most popular recipe since 1978 – but be under no illusions: while it makes the most of the produce native to Jamaica, it's a cake developed with American palates in mind. As Riaz Phillips details in* West Winds*, his book on Jamaican culture and cuisine: 'at the numerous bakeries, high-street, industrial and even hole-in-the-wall shacks (in Jamaica), sweet snacks like gizzadas and toto fly off the shelf quicker than slices of the hummingbird cake.'*

Serves 10

80g (3oz) pecans, toasted and
    roughly chopped
320g (11oz/2½ cups) plain
    (all-purpose) flour
¾ tsp bicarbonate of soda
    (baking soda)
½ tsp baking powder
1 tsp ground cinnamon
½ tsp ground allspice
1 tsp ground ginger
60g (2½oz/¾ cup)
    desiccated (unsweetened
    shredded) coconut
2 large ripe bananas (around
    240g/8¾oz peeled weight)
2 tsp vanilla bean paste (or extract)
½ tsp fine sea salt
200g (7oz) tinned
    pineapple chunks
280g (10oz/1⅓ cups) caster
    (superfine) or granulated sugar
2 large eggs
2cm (¾in) piece of fresh root ginger,
    finely grated
240ml (8fl oz/1 cup) rapeseed oil
    (or another neutral oil)
dried pineapple flowers,
    to decorate

for the icing
2 x 260g (9½oz) packs of cream
    cheese, at room temperature
250g (9oz) butter, at room
    temperature
100g (3½oz/1 cup) icing
    (confectioners') sugar
75ml (2¾fl oz/scant ⅓ cup)
    runny honey

equipment
2 x 20cm (8in) non-stick
    sandwich cake tins
food processor

1 Preheat the oven to 170°C fan/190°C/375°F/gas 5. Grease the cake
   tins and line the bases with circles of greaseproof paper. This is a good
   time to toast the pecans, if you haven't already – they'll take around
   10 minutes in the oven. Once cool, roughly chop them.

2 In a medium bowl, sift together the flour, raising agents and spices,
   then stir through the coconut. In a separate small bowl, mash together
   the bananas, vanilla and salt. Set aside.

3 Drain the pineapple, saving 3 tablespoons of the juice. Briefly pulse
   the chunks in a food processor (or similar) until roughly puréed.

4 In a large bowl, whisk together the sugar, eggs and ginger until
   combined, then gradually pour in the oil, whisking continuously.
   Whisk in the mashed banana, blended pineapple and pineapple
   juice, then fold in the flour mixture, followed by the chopped pecans.

5 Divide the batter between the two cake tins (you can fill the tins quite
   close to the edge, but if there's a little too much batter, pour the excess
   into lined muffin tins). Bake until an inserted skewer comes out clean,
   around 35–45 minutes (it can be helpful to swap the tins over halfway
   through the cooking time, as there's usually a spot in the oven that
   is hotter). Once out of the oven, let the cakes cool completely.

6 For the icing, beat the cream cheese until light and smooth. Separately,
   beat together the butter, icing sugar and honey until light and airy. Whisk
   the two mixes together, divide equally between two bowls, then store
   in the fridge until ready to use.

7 To assemble the cake, cut each cake in half laterally (I find it easiest
   to do this with a serrated bread knife – take it slowly!). Place a cake layer
   on the cake stand or plate that you want to serve the cake on and
   spread a third of the icing (from one bowl) on the top, right to the edge.
   Repeat with the next three layers of cake (the final layer will be naked
   and you will have used all the icing from the first bowl).

8 To ice the cake, take your second bowl of icing and tip half onto the
   top of the cake. Use a spatula to spread the icing over the top and
   sides. Chill in the fridge (or freezer) until the frosting has firmed up,
   around 20–30 minutes (this is called a crumb-coat – it's not essential,
   but it will ensure a neater finish to your icing). Use the remaining icing
   to evenly coat the sides and top of the cake. Decorate with dried
   pineapple flowers.

Tip Topping cakes with a circle of greaseproof paper can help them rise more
evenly, which is particularly useful for cakes that you're planning to stack.
See also: Mango, Coconut + Lime Layer Cake (page 128).

blackened bananas with coconut, passionfruit + ginger

Be sure to place your coconut milk in the fridge overnight.

This is also great cooked on a barbecue and can very easily be scaled up.

balancing elements
passionfruit (sour)
ginger (hot, subtly bitter)

A classic retro pudding like the banana split might look fabulous, but I've always wondered why no effort was ever made to cook the bananas? Cooked bananas are infinitely more delicious than raw ones as heat softens their texture and gently intensifies their sweetness. Let me present to you, then, these roasted bananas: a dessert which is more modern than retro, and more bright than garish, but ultimately – with its flavour and temperature contrasts – turns out to be just as fun as a classic split (and, dare I say, much more delicious).

Serves 4

4 medium ripe bananas
2 tbsp maple syrup
flaky sea salt

for the coconut cream
½ x 400ml (14fl oz) tin of coconut milk, fridge-cold
100ml (3½fl oz/generous ⅓ cup) double (heavy) cream
1 tbsp icing (confectioners') sugar
1 tsp vanilla bean paste

to decorate
3 ripe passionfruit, pulp removed
3 tbsp crystallised ginger, roughly chopped
sweetened coconut flakes (store-bought, e.g. Urban Fruit) (optional)

1 Preheat the oven to 220°C fan/240°C/475°F/gas 9. Line a baking tray with foil.

2 Place the bananas on the prepared tray and use a small knife to slice a slit along two-thirds of the length of each banana. Press the ends of the bananas towards each other to slightly to open up the split, then pour ½ tablespoon of maple syrup into each, followed by a generous pinch of flaky sea salt. Roast the bananas until the skins have turned totally black and they are soft in the middle, around 20 minutes. Remove from the oven and set aside to cool slightly.

3 While the bananas are baking, remove the tin of coconut milk from the fridge and scoop out the top, thicker half into a bowl. Whip up until just shy of soft peaks. Separately, whip together the double cream, icing sugar and vanilla to stiff peaks. Fold the double cream into the coconut cream and whip further, if needed, to thicken it up.

4 To serve, transfer the bananas (still in their skins) to a serving platter, top each with a spoonful of the coconut cream, followed by a teaspoon or two of passionfruit pulp. Garnish with crystallised ginger and coconut flakes (if using) and serve immediately.

crêpes with plantain + rum caramel

When picking out your plantain, opt for fruit that is black and has a soft, squishy texture.

balancing elements
dark rum (subtly bitter)
crème fraîche (sour/tangy)
caramel (bitter/sweet)

Crêpes, bananas and caramel: excellent. So it follows that crêpes, plantain and caramel would also be excellent – and they are! This method of cooking plantain, `plátanos maduros horneados´, is a Central and South American side dish typically served with dairy (e.g. cream cheese or sour cream). Here it works just as well in the context of dessert, and the crème fraîche served alongside not only nods to the original dish but also contributes essential tang to cut through all the sweetness.

Serves 6–8

3 eggs
75g (3oz/generous ⅓ cup)
   caster (superfine) sugar
500ml (17fl oz/generous 2 cups)
   whole milk
250g (9oz/2 cups) plain
   (all-purpose) flour
½ tsp fine sea salt
1 tbsp rum (optional)
20g (¾oz) butter, melted,
   plus extra for cooking

for the plantain
2 very ripe plantain
1 tbsp maple syrup
100ml (3½fl oz/generous
   ⅓ cup) water
1 tbsp/15g butter, softened
2 tbsp light muscovado
   (or light brown) sugar

for the rum caramel sauce
200g (7oz/1 cup)
   caster (superfine) sugar
2 tbsp double (heavy) cream
2 tbsp dark rum
30g (1oz) butter
1 tsp vanilla bean paste
½ tsp flaky sea salt
crème fraîche, to serve

equipment
baking dish to snugly
   fit the plantain
crêpe pan (or frying pan/skillet)

1. Preheat the oven to 160°C fan/180°C/350°F/gas 4.

2. Make the crêpe batter by whisking together the eggs and caster sugar, along with 100ml (3½fl oz/generous ⅓ cup) of the milk. Next, whisk in the flour and salt, but don't worry about lumps. Gradually add the rest of the milk, incorporating it a third at a time until you have a fairly liquid batter. Whisk in the rum (if using) and melted butter. Sieve the batter to get rid of any lumps and set aside to rest.

3. Cut the plantain in half lengthways, then peel off the skin. Add the plantain to the baking dish, cut sides up, then pour over the maple syrup and water, and dot the butter around. Cover with foil and bake in the oven for 45 minutes until really soft. Next, sprinkle over the light muscovado sugar and turn up the heat to 200°C fan/220°C/425°F/gas 7. Bake (uncovered) for a further 15 minutes until the sugar has caramelised, then remove from the oven.

4. Meanwhile, make the rum caramel sauce by cooking the sugar over a medium heat until it has fully melted and you have a fluid, clear, amber caramel. Whisk in the double cream until incorporated, followed by the rum. Allow to simmer for a couple of minutes before removing from the heat and whisking in the butter, vanilla and salt. Cover and place over the lowest heat to keep warm until ready to serve.

5. Heat a crêpe pan (or frying pan) to a high heat. Add a small knob of butter and allow it to melt, then use some kitchen paper to wipe it around the pan. Pour 50ml (2fl oz/scant ¼ cup) of the batter into the pan, tilting it to ensure an even crêpe. Cook until the underside takes on a golden colour – this should take no more than a minute or so – then flip it and allow to cook on the second side for 30 seconds. Remove from the pan and keep the crêpes stacked on a plate covered by a tea towel.

6. To serve, fold each crêpe into quarters, then transfer one or two to a serving plate. Add pieces of caramelised plantain, a spoonful of crème fraîche and a generous drizzle of the rum caramel sauce.

Tip Most batters – whether for Yorkshire puddings, crêpes, blinis, etc. – benefit from some resting time before cooking, as this allows the flour to properly absorb the liquid. See also: Russian Honey (Crêpe) Cake (page 168).

banana, chocolate + tahini brioche pudding

Don't skip on the bain-marie, as it ensures a perfect texture.

Do make sure you use a silky Middle Eastern tahini for this.

I would like to be 'relaxed' and say that the date molasses is just a serving suggestion, but I think its tangy sweetness takes this to another level – I like Odysea's.

balancing elements
semi-sweet chocolate (subtly bitter)
tahini (subtly bitter)
date molasses (sweet/sour)

I'm not generally a fan of tahini in sweet contexts, but even I am frankly obsessed with the combination of banana, chocolate and tahini in just about any form – it's truly one of the great flavour pairings. And while it's a combination that might sound a little out there for a bread-and-butter pudding, I assure you that this version retains all the comforting, gentle qualities that you would rightly expect, all while providing a little extra oomph.

Serves 6–8

1 x 500g (1lb 2oz) brioche loaf, stale and sliced
2 bananas, peeled and roughly chopped
90g (3¼oz) semi-sweet chocolate chips (at least 46% cocoa solids; higher if you prefer bitter flavours – I like Guittard)
250ml (8½fl oz/generous 1 cup) double (heavy) cream
500ml (17fl oz/generous 2 cups) milk
90g (3¼oz/scant ½ cup) caster (superfine) sugar
2 tsp vanilla bean paste
5 egg yolks
100g (3½oz/7 tbsp) Middle Eastern tahini
date molasses, to serve

equipment
baking dish, about 27 x 34cm (11 x 14in) (or similar)
larger roasting tin, for the baking dish to sit in

1   Preheat the oven to 150°C fan/170°C/340°F/gas 3.

2   Cut the brioche slices into quarters and scatter into the baking dish, sprinkling the chopped banana and chocolate chips in among them (don't leave the banana or chocolate too exposed on the top of the pudding as they will burn when baking).

3   In a saucepan, heat the cream, milk, half of the sugar and the vanilla together until the mixture comes to a boil, then remove from the heat immediately.

4   Separately, whisk together the egg yolks and remaining sugar in a medium bowl, followed by the tahini. Slowly whisk in the cream mixture, a quarter at time, then gently pour the tahini custard over the brioche and leave it to soak for 20 minutes.

5   Place the dish in the roasting tin and pour boiling water until it reaches two-thirds up the side. Bake until set and golden on top, around 50 minutes–1 hour. Allow to cool for 10–15 minutes before serving with a drizzle of date molasses.

Tip The bain-marie technique – though rarely essential – is the best way to guarantee a gentle cook on any kind of custard-based dessert or cheesecake, guaranteeing you a smooth set and minimising the risk of cracks. See also: Little Vanilla Bean Pots with Plums, page 138.

banoffee coffee sundae

I've included a recipe for a no-churn ice cream, which would need to be made the day before you intend to serve, but store-bought coffee ice cream would also work brilliantly in this recipe. Likewise with the caramel sauce.

The majority of the elements can be prepared in advance, but it's best to whip up the cream at the last minute.

balancing elements
coffee (bitter)
cocoa nibs (bitter)
salted caramel (bitter/salty/sweet)
dark rum (subtly bitter)
cardamom (subtly bitter)

The best dinner party recipes are ones that maximise fun for the guests and minimise stress for the host – and this is one of those. I say this with confidence: a make-your-own-sundae situation at the end of a dinner party will never grow old (we are all children at heart). In this case, you'll recognise the elements of a banoffee pie, made a little more grown up with some bitter flavours (espresso ice cream, a splash of rum, cocoa nibs). Place all the elements down the middle of the table, and let your guests get creative.

Serves 4–6

12 digestive biscuits (Graham crackers)
1 x quantity of caramel sauce (page 60, or store-bought)
4 ripe bananas, peeled and cut into 1cm (½in) thick slices on the bias
cocoa nibs, to decorate

for the espresso no-churn ice cream
300ml (10fl oz/1¼ cups) double (heavy) cream, fridge-cold
175g (6oz/generous ¾ cup) condensed milk
2 tbsp instant espresso powder (I use Nescafé)
2 tbsp dark rum
¼ tsp ground cardamom

for the cinnamon cream
150ml (5fl oz/⅔ cup) double (heavy) cream, fridge-cold
¼–½ tsp ground cinnamon, to taste

equipment
sundae glasses/dessert coupes/bowls

1 To make the ice cream, whisk together all the ingredients in a medium bowl until the mixture reaches soft peaks. Transfer to a freezer-proof container and freeze overnight.

2 To make the cinnamon cream, whip the double cream and ground cinnamon to soft peaks.

3 To serve, present all the different elements in bowls down the middle of the table and allow everyone to make up their own sundaes. Here's how I would compile mine: crush a couple of digestive biscuits into the bottom of a sundae glass, spoon over some caramel sauce, then top with slices of banana. Add a scoop of the espresso ice cream, followed by a spoonful of the cinnamon cream, then drizzle over more caramel sauce and shower with cocoa nibs.

strawberries

The strawberry, with its bright scarlet hue and heady scent, is the quintessential British berry. Many will associate it with the iconic Wimbledon, or summer garden parties, but for me they conjure memories of strawberry picking near my grandparents' farm. Regardless of context, the top-heavy, juicy strawberry – with its tiny seeds peppering the outside – is a fruit that says, emphatically: 'Come and eat me.' And who are we to refuse?

Strawberries have long grown wild across the temperate regions of the world, but for hundreds of years they were very small (similar to today's *fraise de bois*, 'woodland strawberries'). At this size, they never became more than a tiny, flavourful delicacy enjoyed occasionally (and sometimes ostentatiously) by the upper classes: Madame Tallien, a prominent figure at the court of Napoleon, would sometimes bathe in their juices, while it's reported that strawberries were Louis XIV's favourite fruit.

It was only when the strawberry was domesticated in Chile, achieving much bigger berries, that the strawberry's potential began to manifest. Amédée-François Frézier, a military engineer, discovered the Chilean strawberry while on a mission in the Spanish-held commune of Concepción. Employed by Louis XIV to collect intelligence related to the War of the Spanish Succession, Frézier was clearly destined to play a role in the history of the *fraise* (strawberry) on account of his name. He must have known of Louis XIV's love for the fruit, because he brought back five strawberry plants from his travels, one of which he kept, giving the others away. For years the plants bore no fruit because most strawberry species are single sex. It wasn't until the early 1600s, when the Virginia species of strawberry made its way to Europe, that the Virginia strawberry and Chilean strawberry were planted together, and started to mate. Suddenly, there were gluts of strawberries all over France and they transformed from small treats reserved for royals to big, aromatic berries available to the masses at open-air markets. Cultivated strawberries subsequently spread around the globe.

Today, strawberry flavour exists everywhere – in snack foods, soft drinks, cosmetics – and yet they're a highly seasonal fruit: the difference between a height-of-summer British strawberry and a greenhouse-grown specimen is night and day. I can't deny the delights of a homemade strawberry jam, or a tub of strawberry ice cream – but when perfectly ripe, strawberries need no cooking: a flawless strawberry is nature's perfect candy. And if you acquire some berries that are not quite ripe enough, or a bit underwhelming, then maceration (a brief toss with sugar and lemon juice or vinegar) can achieve miracles. For this chapter, I have created a set of recipes that introduce strawberries to exciting flavours, which can be used not only at the peak of summer but also whenever you can't get your hands on the perfect berries (or – shhhh – when you want to eat them out of season).

If strawberries lack anything, it is the acidity found in most other berries (raspberries, blackberries, etc.). Alone they are perfect, but the addition of too much sugar makes them redolent of candy floss (cotton candy). What works best is finding ways to balance out strawberries' inherent sweetness: the soothing effect of dairy (see Strawberries + Cream Cake, page 76), the surprise of a little spice (see Strawberry + Pepper 'Marvellous' Cakes, page 84), the addition of some acidity (see Rice Pudding Soufflé Cake with Sumac Strawberries, page 93). These small adjustments ensure that strawberries shine as brightly in your desserts as they do eaten, without adornment, on a glorious summer's day.

strawberries + cream cake

This cake is very versatile – you can swap the strawberries for other berries (e.g. raspberries) or stone fruit (e.g. apricots).

Because of the moisture of the strawberries, the cake may have a pudding-like texture in places.

balancing elements
buttermilk (sour)
lemon zest (bitter)

I don't have all that much time for a cooked strawberry, but you know what? Sometimes your strawberries aren't that sweet. Or they're on their last legs. Or, heaven forbid, you just want to enjoy some strawberries out of season. And when these moments arise, there is no more fitting way to use them than in this cake which, somehow, tastes like the fairground.

Serves 6–8 people

125ml (4¼fl oz/½ cup) buttermilk
125ml (4¼fl oz/½ cup) double
    (heavy) cream
80g (3oz) butter
140g (5oz/⅔ cup) caster (superfine)
    or granulated sugar
zest of 1 lemon
¼ tsp fine sea salt
2 eggs
150g (5oz/1 cup plus 2 tbsp)
    self-raising flour
250g (9oz) strawberries,
    hulled and halved
    (quartered if particularly large)
1 tbsp demerara
    (turbinado) sugar
½ tsp ground cinnamon

equipment
20cm (8in) non-stick loose-
    bottomed/springform cake tin
electric hand whisk

1   Preheat the oven to 170°C fan/190°C/375°F/gas 5 and line the base of your tin with a circle of greaseproof paper.

2   Combine the buttermilk and double cream in a jug or small bowl.

3   In a large bowl, cream together the butter, sugar, lemon zest and salt until light and fluffy, at least 5 minutes. Add in the eggs, one at a time, beating thoroughly between each addition and scraping down the bowl. Briefly whisk in half of the flour (until mostly incorporated), followed by half of the buttermilk-cream mixture. Repeat until you have a homogenous batter (but avoid overmixing). Fold through half of the strawberries.

4   Transfer the batter to the prepared cake tin. Level it off as best you can with an offset spatula (or back of a spoon), then press the remaining strawberry halves into the top, cut-sides up. Mix together the demerara sugar and cinnamon, then sprinkle this over the top of the cake.

5   Bake until the top is deeply golden, the cake is pulling away from the sides of the tin and an inserted skewer comes out clean, around 50 minutes–1 hour.

Tip Adding a richer dairy product, such as ricotta, sour cream or double (heavy) cream to a cake batter will make for a plusher, softer crumb (due to the higher fat and moisture content), as well as help the cake keep well for longer. Next time you're making a Victoria sponge, try adding double cream in lieu of milk, until the cake reaches dropping consistency. See also: Blackcurrant, Bay + Clotted Cream Cake (page 163) and French Yoghurt Pot Loaf (page 160).

Tip To make 'faux' buttermilk, simply combine 100ml (3½fl oz/generous ⅓ cup) whole milk with 2 tbsp fresh lemon juice. See also: Date, Fennel Seed + Lemon Scones (page 200).

matcha
tiramisu

This requires 24 hours in the fridge before eating, which makes it a perfect dinner party dessert.

For a double-layered tiramisu (my preference), you will need a dish that's at least 6cm (2½in) in height and about 24 x 19cm (9½ x 7½in). Alternatively, you can make this recipe as a single-layer tiramisu in a typical 23 x 33cm (9 x 13in) baking dish.

balancing elements
matcha (bitter)
balsamic vinegar (sour/sweet)
amaretto (subtly bitter)

This is proof that we can all change – that the ideas and beliefs we held steadfast to yesterday may not serve us today, or tomorrow. I have always been adamant that no one should mess with tiramisu. A masterpiece of bitterness balanced with sweetness, when someone decides to go rogue and add orange, or cherries or hazelnuts to it . . . I get upset. And yet, here I am, presenting you with a 'tiramisu' that has zero authenticity.

This recipe takes the concept of tiramisu (soaked savoiardi biscuits, layered with a sabayon-like cream) and pushes it in a completely different direction: intensely bitter espresso becomes grassy, bitter matcha, while the strawberries offer sweetness, colour and freshness. It's a tiramisu that's holidaying in Japan, I guess? Whatever it is, it's delicious.

Serves 8–10

100g (3½oz/scant ½ cup) caster (superfine) sugar
4 eggs, separated
500g (1lb 2oz) mascarpone
2 tbsp amaretto
120ml (4fl oz/½ cup) double (heavy) cream, fridge-cold

for the balsamic strawberries
300g (10½oz) strawberries, chopped quite finely
2 tsp caster (superfine) sugar
1 tsp balsamic vinegar

for the tea
500ml (17fl oz/generous 2 cups) hot water
25g (1oz) premium-grade matcha powder
2 tsp vanilla bean paste

to assemble
matcha powder, for dusting between the layers
200g (7oz) savoiardi biscuits (sponge fingers)

equipment
electric hand whisk
23 x 33cm (9 x 13in) baking dish (for single layer) or 24 x 19cm (9½ x 7½in) dish, at least 6cm (2½in) tall (for double layer)

1 For the balsamic strawberries, combine the strawberries with the sugar and balsamic vinegar, then set aside to macerate.

2 Separately, whisk together the hot water, matcha power and vanilla bean paste for the tea. Set aside.

3 To make the cream for the tiramisu, add the sugar and egg yolks to a large bowl. Whisk for a couple of minutes using an electric whisk until the mixture has paled and thickened. Separately, whisk the mascarpone until smooth and lump-free, then whisk this into the egg mixture along with the amaretto. In a separate bowl, whisk the egg whites to stiff peaks, then fold gently into the mascarpone mixture, half at a time. In the egg white bowl, whisk the double cream until it holds, then fold this into the mascarpone mixture.

4 To assemble, dust the base of the baking dish with matcha powder. Scatter half the strawberries over the base (or the full amount if making the single-layered tiramisu). Dip the sponge fingers in the tea for 2–3 seconds, then lay in a single layer across the bottom of the dish. Cover with half of the mascarpone cream (or the full amount if making the single-layered version). Dust liberally with matcha powder and repeat to add a second layer, leaving the last cream layer bare. Chill in the fridge for at least 24 hours.

5 Dust with matcha powder just before serving.

Tip Always give any tiramisu (and most trifles!) a minimum of 24 hours – but ideally 48 – for the flavours and textures to meld together. It makes a huge difference to the final result.

asha's japanese strawberry shortcake

This is a cake to make when you have time to bake. Take plenty of care: follow the instructions exactly and take shortcuts at your peril (I learnt this the hard way)!

Freeze-dried strawberries are typically cheaper purchased from a health food store or online, instead of a supermarket.

balancing element
freeze-dried strawberries (sour)

Japanese shortcake is a cake made of the lightest, airiest sponge, sandwiched with freshly whipped cream and strawberries – not so dissimilar to a French fraisier, but lighter and less sweet. My friend Asha loves Japanese culture and has long turned out beautiful Japanese shortcakes for birthdays and celebrations (based on a recipe by Namiko Hirasaw Chen). Here I've adapted it with a strawberry cream twist that adds additional fruity, tart flavour.

Serves 10–12

45g (1¾oz) butter, at room temperature, plus extra for greasing
130g (4½oz/1 cup) cake flour (or 110g/4oz/scant 1 cup plain/all-purpose flour plus 1 generous tbsp cornflour/ cornstarch)
2 tbsp whole milk
4 large eggs, at room temperature
100g (3½oz/½ cup) caster (superfine) sugar

for the strawberry cream
20g (¾oz) freeze-dried strawberries
100g (3½oz/½ cup) caster (superfine) sugar
80ml (3fl oz/⅓ cup) whole milk
400ml (13fl oz/1⅔ cups) double (heavy) cream, fridge-cold

to decorate
300g (10½oz) strawberries, hulled and quartered, plus 15–17 strawberries of the same height, hulled and halved vertically

equipment
temperature probe
electric hand whisk
food processor
20cm (8in) silicone cake tin (or a non-stick springform cake tin)
acetate cake collar

1 Preheat the oven to 180°C fan/200°C/400°F/gas 6. If using a springform tin, turn the base upside down so that there is no lip around the edge and line with greaseproof paper. If you have it, spray the edges with cake release spray (to ensure the neatest edge) – or alternatively grease the sides with butter. Sift the cake flour into a small bowl.

2 Bring a medium saucepan half-filled with water to a gentle simmer. Place a small heatproof bowl on top (the bowl should not touch the water). Add the butter to the bowl and leave to melt. Whisk the milk into the butter, then set the bowl aside with your temperature probe in the mixture. Keep half an eye on it – you want it to come down to 40°C (104°F). Leave the pan of water on the stove but turn the heat off.

3 In a large bowl, use the electric whisk to briefly break up the eggs (20 seconds), then add the sugar and whisk to combine (20 seconds). When the water in the pan on the stove has reached 60°C (140°F), put it back over a low heat and place the bowl with the eggs and sugar over the top. Whisk until the mixture reaches 40°C (104°F). At this point, take the bowl off the pan of water and whisk the eggs on high speed until the mixture is pale, fluffy and glossy, around 3 minutes. The egg mixture should have tripled in volume and reached ribbon stage.

4 Sift half of the flour into the egg mixture, then use a metal spoon to very gently fold the flour through. It is incredibly important that the flour is combined thoroughly – make sure you go all around the bowl including the base to pick up all the pockets of flour. Repeat with the rest of the flour.

5 Take out a large spoonful of batter from the bowl and add it to the melted butter mixture. Whisk to combine. Next, pour a third of this mixture down the side of the egg mixture, over the back of a spoon to ensure that it's added very gently, and gently fold it through. Repeat with the rest of the mixture.

6 Pour the sponge mixture into your prepared cake tin, keeping your bowl low to avoid incorporating more air. Tap the tin on the counter to release any air bubbles. Bake for 20–25 minutes until a skewer inserted into the middle of the cake comes out clean. Allow to cool for 10 minutes before removing from the tin.

7 Make the strawberry cream only when you're ready to assemble the cake (and when the cakes have completely cooled). First, blend the freeze-dried strawberries and sugar in a food processor until powdery. In a separate bowl, add the strawberry sugar and milk to the cream and whip until just shy of soft peaks. You can let it down with a bit more milk, if needed.

8 To assemble the cake, get the plate or stand that you want to serve it on and place the empty springform tin (closed, without its base) on top. Slice the cold sponge in half horizontally to make 2 thin, even discs. Place the acetate collar around the inside of the tin, then set one sponge disc inside, cut side up, gently squashing the edges of the cake down so that they are pushed directly against the sides of the tin. Arrange the halved strawberries around the edge on top of the sponge layer, pointed ends up and cut sides against the acetate, making sure they are fitted snugly next to each other. You should have a few strawberry halves left over for decorating the top. Spoon a third of the strawberry cream into the centre of the cake, then use a palette knife to smooth it over, encouraging the cream between the strawberries to fill all the gaps. Spoon the quartered strawberries evenly over the cream, then top with another third of the cream, spreading it out until level with the palette knife. Set the other disc of sponge on top, cut side down, and gently press down so that the assembled cake is firmly pressed against the acetate all round. Top the cake with clouds of the remaining cream and arrange the remaining halved strawberries on top.

9 To serve, release the sides of the cake tin, then gently remove the acetate. The cake can be chilled for a cleaner slice, although I prefer to serve this straightaway.

the neo neapolitan

To ensure a good strawberry flavour, make this with height-of-season strawberries. Outside of strawberry season I would opt for raspberries.

While the small amount of vodka in this recipe helps to keep the ice cream soft (see tip on page 90), it can be left out if you need something alcohol-free.

Although the crystallised pistachios add beauty and texture, they can be left out for the sake of simplicity!

Get the ice cream out of the freezer around 10–15 minutes before serving to allow it to soften a little.

balancing elements
crème fraîche (sour/tangy)
vodka (bitter)
lemon zest (bitter)

The creation of Neapolitan ice cream was a boon for bickering families – each individual could mine their favourite – but, arguably, a fail on the flavour front. I don't know about you, but I'm pretty sure that vanilla, strawberry and chocolate don't go together. In this redo, pistachios step in to bring the indulgence (bye, chocolate) and crème fraîche offers tang to the vanilla layer – both flavours that work beautifully alongside strawberries.

Makes around 8 slices

for the pistachio layer
50g (2oz/¼ cup) caster (superfine) sugar
50ml (2fl oz/3 tbsp plus 1 tsp) water
50g (2oz) pistachios
50g (2oz) smooth, store-bought pistachio paste
1 tbsp vodka (see tip, below)
250ml (8½fl oz/generous 1 cup) double (heavy) cream, fridge-cold
2 tbsp icing (confectioners') sugar

for the strawberry layer
200g (7oz) strawberries, halved
100g (3½oz/½ cup) caster (superfine) sugar
juice of ½ lemon
1 tbsp vodka (see tip, below)
300ml (10fl oz/1⅓ cups) double (heavy) cream, fridge-cold
2 tbsp icing (confectioners') sugar

for the crème fraîche layer
160g (5½oz/⅔ cup) crème fraîche, fridge-cold
2 tbsp icing (confectioners') sugar
zest of ½ lemon
200ml (7fl oz/generous ¾ cup) double (heavy) cream, fridge-cold
1 tsp vanilla bean paste

equipment
900g (2lb) loaf tin, lined with cling film (plastic wrap), allowing a decent overhang on each side
stick blender (or standard blender)

1 Start by making the crystallised pistachios. Line a baking tray with greaseproof paper. Bring the sugar and water to a boil in a small saucepan (do not stir) and wait for the mixture to turn golden at the edges. Add the pistachios and stir vigorously until the sugar crystallises around the nuts and everything turns dry. Turn out onto the baking tray. Once cool, break up into individual crystallised nuts, then lightly chop.

2 Next, make the strawberry compote. Remove a quarter of the strawberries and chop them into 7mm (¼in) cubes (or roughly, if you prefer). Gently simmer the rest of the strawberries, sugar and lemon juice in a small pan for 6–8 minutes until the berries are starting to break down. Use a stick blender (or standard blender) to purée the cooked strawberries, then pass through a sieve. Set aside.

3 For the pistachio layer, whisk together the pistachio paste and vodka in a medium bowl (the mixture may seize up, but don't worry). In a separate bowl (and with a clean whisk), whip the double cream and icing sugar to soft peaks. Add a spoonful or two of the cream into the pistachio mix and whisk to loosen. Fold in the rest of the cream until the mixture is smooth and uniform, then fold in the crystallised pistachios. Pour into the prepared loaf tin to a depth of about a third (you may have a little mix left over) and smooth over with a small offset spatula (or back of a spoon). Place in the freezer for 1–1½ hours.

4 For the crème fraîche layer, whisk together the crème fraîche, icing sugar and lemon zest in a medium bowl. Separately, whip the double cream and vanilla to soft peaks. Fold the double cream through the crème fraîche mixture until smooth. Spoon the mixture over the pistachio layer in the tin up to about two-thirds full (you may have a little mix left over), smoothing the top as before. Return to the freezer for 1–1½ hours.

Recipe continues overleaf

5   Finally, make the strawberry layer. In a small bowl, stir together the strawberry compote and vodka. In a separate bowl, whip the double cream and icing sugar to soft peaks. Whisk a spoonful of the whipped double cream into the strawberry mixture to loosen it, then gently fold in the rest of the double cream, followed by the chopped fresh strawberries. Pour the mixture over the crème fraiche layer in the tin and smooth the top as before. Return to the freezer for at least 3 hours, or overnight.

6   To serve, unpeel the cling film from the top and lift out the ice cream brick. Unwrap and cut into slabs.

Tip While never essential, vodka can be a useful ingredient: it inhibits gluten formation in batters and doughs where you want to preserve lightness or flakiness; it inhibits crystallisation in ice creams and sorbets (helpful for the no-churn variety, such as this one); and it is also a flavour carrier (hence why penne alla vodka is so well-loved). See also: No Churn Dulce De Leche Ice Cream (page 167).

rouge summer pudding

This requires an overnight stint in the fridge.

Serve with cold double (heavy) cream.

If you'd like to make this vegan, simply use ordinary soft white bread instead of brioche, plant-based butter, and serve with a plant-based cream.

balancing elements
redcurrants (sour)
raspberries (sour/tart)
lemon peel (bitter)

I can't describe the classic British summer pudding more charmingly than Olivia Potts: 'It is a pudding which defies gravity and sense, and rewards faith . . . it is elegant in its simplicity, (yet) it seems distinctly British to name soggy, stale bread stuffed with fruit after an entire season.' Summer pudding typically contains sour blackcurrants, but the Danish red berry pudding, rødgrød med fløde, inspired me to stick to the red kind for this recipe, which explains its crimson colour and brighter flavour.

Serves 6

900g (2lb) mixed red summer berries (I like 400g/14oz strawberries, quartered, 250g/9oz raspberries, 200g/7oz cherries, halved and pitted, and 150g/5oz redcurrants), plus extra to serve
2 tbsp caster (superfine) sugar
2 tbsp water
1 strip of fresh lemon peel
1–2 tbsp rose water, to taste
butter, for greasing
around 8–9 slices of brioche (or soft white bread), crusts removed
double (heavy) cream, to serve

equipment
1 litre (1¾ pint) pudding basin or Pyrex bowl

1   Combine the berries, sugar, water and lemon peel in a saucepan and leave to macerate for 30 minutes. Simmer over a medium-low heat for 5–7 minutes until syrupy, then add the rose water to taste. Set aside to cool completely, then strain the berries from the juice (keeping both).

2   Butter your basin, then cut 6 of the brioche slices to fit into the sides (I find cutting them in half lengthways, but slightly on an angle is best). Build up the sides by dipping the pieces of brioche into the syrup, then placing the thinner end of the bread towards the centre (there will be a hole left in the middle). Overlap each piece slightly and press to seal. Once the sides have been built, take another slice of brioche and cut a circle that's just slightly bigger than the remaining space. Dip in the berry syrup and place at the bottom of the bowl, pressing to seal.

3   Spoon the drained berries into the centre of the pudding, leaving a gap of 1cm (½in) at the top and adding an extra tablespoon or two of the berry syrup. Use the final piece of brioche to cut a round that will fit just inside the sides. Dip this piece into the berry syrup and then place on top of the filling. Fold over the bread ends and press down to seal. Cover the top with cling film (plastic wrap), then weigh it down with a small plate, adding some weights on top if you have them. Place in the fridge overnight. Strain any remaining berry syrup (to get rid of crumbs) and store in the fridge for serving.

4   To serve, turn the pudding out onto a serving plate and garnish with fresh berries, if liked. Serve slices with a generous pour of double (heavy) cream (or a plant-based equivalent) and a little extra berry syrup.

rice pudding soufflé cake with sumac strawberries

I find it easiest to make the rice pudding the night before.

You could double the rice pudding recipe to have rice pudding for dessert, and then make this the next day (but keep the salt quantity at ½ teaspoon when doubling).

The strawberries can be made a couple of days ahead and stored in a sealed container in the fridge.

To make this dairy free, swap the whole milk for rice milk, the double cream for oat cream and leave out the butter.

balancing elements
sumac (sour)
lemon peel (bitter)
amaretto (subtly bitter)
salt

Italian torta di riso presumably came about from a need to use up leftover rice pudding, although I've never been able to work out how that would happen. Still, if you ever wanted to deliver the childish pleasures of a nursery-school classic in an altogether more chic and adult guise, then this is the recipe for you. Classic torta di riso recipes are, I'll be honest, too dense for my taste, so in this version extra whipped egg whites result in a lighter, more soufflé-like texture. The sour-sweet sumac strawberries bring the strawberry 'jam' part of the equation, and when I tell you they are knockout . . .

Serves 8–10

for the rice pudding
625ml (1 pint plus 2 tbsp/2⅔ cups) whole milk
150ml (5fl oz/⅔ cup) double (heavy) cream
2 tbsp caster (superfine) or granulated sugar
1 pared strip of lemon zest
2 pared strips of orange zest
½ tsp fine sea salt
165g (5½oz/¾ cup) pudding rice
1 tsp vanilla bean paste
25g (1oz) butter, plus extra for greasing the tin
1 tbsp amaretto
 (or ¼ tsp almond essence)

for the strawberries
720g (1lb 9½oz) strawberries, hulled and kept whole (halved if large)
3 tbsp caster (superfine) or granulated sugar
1½ tbsp sumac

for the cake
5 egg whites, at room temperature
90g (3¼oz/scant ½ cup) caster (superfine) or granulated sugar
3 egg yolks, at room temperature

equipment
20cm (8in) non-stick springform cake tin
baking dish (large enough to fit the strawberries in a single layer)
electric hand whisk

1   To make the rice pudding, place the milk, cream, sugar, zests and salt in a saucepan and heat until steaming. Add the rice and bring to a simmer. Allow it to bubble away gently, giving it a stir every minute or so initially, then less frequently as the mixture thickens. Cook until the rice has only a slight bite and the mixture is thick and creamy, around 20–25 minutes. Remove from the heat, then beat in the vanilla, butter and amaretto. Transfer the rice pudding to a bowl and leave to cool.

2   Preheat the oven to 140°C fan/160°C/325°F/gas 3. Grease and line the base of the cake tin with greaseproof paper.

3   Prepare the strawberries by tossing them in the sugar and sumac, then spread them out on a baking dish lined with greaseproof paper (or a silicone baking mat). Set aside.

4   In a large clean bowl, whisk the egg whites to stiff peaks with an electric hand whisk. Add the sugar a heaped tablespoon at a time and keep whisking until you have a glossy meringue.

5   Stir the egg yolks into the cooled rice pudding, then whisk in a big spoonful of the meringue to loosen its texture. Gently fold half of the remaining meringue into the rice pudding until incorporated, then follow up with the rest.

6   Pour the batter into the prepared tin and transfer to the oven, along with the strawberries which should go on the shelf below. Bake until the cake is lightly golden and puffed up, around 45 minutes. The strawberries should have reduced in size, be looking slightly dried out and sitting in a strawberry syrup – if needed, give them another 10–15 minutes.

7   Allow the cake to cool a little in the tin, then run your knife around the edges and release the sides. I tend to serve it directly from the tin base, but you could attempt to transfer it to a plate – this is more likely to be successful once the cake has been chilled in the fridge. Serve slices still warm with the sumac strawberries spooned over the top (note: this is not a 'perfect slice' cake, it's more rustic than that). This is also excellent cold after an overnight stint in the fridge.

peaches

A ripe peach is the most perfect of perfect things – ambrosial, sweet, drip-down-your-arms juicy. But it's true that you have to be lucky to live where peaches of this quality are regularly available (e.g. Italy, or Georgia in the US). For the rest of us, it's a lottery with slim odds: in a single stretch of summer you would be lucky if you enjoyed one or two such fruits. And when (if) you do, the best course of action is simply to bite into its soft flesh, leaning over a sink to catch the juices as they run down your chin – no embellishments needed. But for the times when hard, underripe peaches are all that you can find, heat is your friend: peaches love to be roasted, griddled, poached – both their texture and colour hold up well under this sort of pressure, and their sweetness intensifies.

You'd be forgiven for not knowing where peaches originated. I initially associated them with the American south (Georgia is known as 'the peach state') and Italy. In fact, even its botanical name – *Prunus persica,* which translates as 'Persian plum' – would lead you astray, because as it so happens peaches are native to China. As early as 6,000 BC, these nectar-like fruits were domesticated in the Zhejiang province, before travelling west via the Silk Route to Persia. The Met's collection holds a sixteenth-century silk tapestry depicting Dongfang Shuo (154–93 BC), an old man, cradling a precious, stolen peach.[1] Entitled *Immortal Holding a Peach*, it forms part of the Taoist belief that eating peaches bestows eternal life. The Chinese classical novel *Journey to the West* features a similar story, where the Monkey King travels the world searching for the immortal peach after seeing another monkey die of old age. Peaches are peppered throughout the Chinese arts, as well as day-to-day life: the Chinese word for peach, *tao,* is used as a name for girls or boys, with the meaning of 'long life'; peaches have significance in Chinese medicine and flew off the shelves in China during the COVID-19 pandemic; and peach blossoms are symbolic around the Chinese New Year and marriage celebrations, where they represent rebirth, love and beauty. All of this to say: peach's roots run deep in Chinese culture.

Fast-forward to the twenty-first century and peaches feature repeatedly, from Roald Dahl's *James and the Giant Peach* (Dahl originally chose a cherry but decided that a peach was juicier) to Princess Peach in Nintendo's Mario franchise; from Justin Bieber's 'Peaches' to the rampant use of the peach emoji all over social media. It might be easy to assume that peaches have only recently become a pop culture fetish, but they have long had a sexualised image: 'bitten peach' was a byword for homosexuality in China, while the women of the American south have for decades been referred to as 'Georgia peaches'. Given peaches' inherent juiciness and shape, I expect they will continue to court this kind of attention.

Peaches vary in shape and type: round or flat; yellow or white-fleshed; sweeter or more acidic; more or less perfumed; floral, creamy, fragrant. But what unites them all is a tactile, fuzzy coat that makes them seem, in some ways, at odds with summer. Flavour-wise, peaches and spice always make something nice: cinnamon, ginger, black pepper and cloves all add a subtle natural warmth that complements peaches' inherent sweetness. This is particularly the case for cloves, as peaches contain eugenol, the identifying flavour compound of cloves – which is to say that: cloves can make peaches taste even more of themselves (see page 100). The combination of peaches and almonds (see page 104), meanwhile, is a poetic one since a peach stone itself has an almond flavour which can be extracted to make syrups or infused into ice cream (although caution is advised as they can contain cyanide compounds). Alcohol is also a natural bedfellow: peach slices in Moscato wine, peaches and bourbon, the now ubiquitous Bellini . . . not to mention the peach notes that turn up in aromatic wines, such as Riesling, Gewürztraminer and Viognier.

But peaches are not just for pudding. The balance of sweet and savoury can be addictive, and peaches are a willing participant. They work well in salads, because they love to be paired with fresh, creamy cheeses (mozzarella, ricotta, soft goat's cheese – see page 210) as well as salty cured hams such as prosciutto. They hold their shape and colour well, so are not liable to going mushy. Their sweetness is also a lovely addition to rich meats such as duck. No peaches? No problem. The beauty of many of the recipes in this chapter is that you can substitute other stone fruit – most obviously nectarines (which are, essentially, the same fruit), but in many cases plums or apricots, too. Still, in the presence of a perfect specimen you'll find it hard to beat peachy perfection.

1   https://www.metmuseum.org/art/collection/search/44059

peachy cornbread pancakes

These pancakes are on the less sweet side because I assume you're going to have them with the sweet blueberry maple sauce – but if that's not the case, simply increase the sugar to 3 or 4 tablespoons.

The blueberry sauce is greater than the sum of its parts – you may want to consider doubling it.

Serve with Greek yoghurt if you'd like something creamy on the side.

balancing elements
buttermilk (sour/tangy)
blueberries (subtly sour)

Makes 10-12 pancakes

30g (1oz) ghee (or butter), melted in the pan you're planning to use for the pancakes, plus extra as needed
2 tbsp caster (superfine) or granulated sugar
1 egg
¼ tsp vanilla bean paste (or extract)
150ml (5fl oz/⅔ cup) buttermilk
½ tsp bicarbonate of soda (baking soda)
½ tsp ground cinnamon
½ tsp fine sea salt
80g (3oz/scant ¾ cup) plain (all-purpose) flour
50g (2oz/scant ½ cup) fine cornmeal
1-2 peaches, halved, pitted and each half sliced into 3mm (⅛in) slices
Greek yoghurt, to serve (optional)

for the blueberry sauce
150g (5oz) blueberries
1 tbsp maple syrup

Peaches, blueberries and cornmeal . . . these are American southern comfort in pancake form.

1   Whisk the melted ghee (or butter), sugar, egg, vanilla and buttermilk in a medium–large bowl until combined. Next, whisk in the bicarbonate of soda, cinnamon and salt. Combine the flour and cornmeal together in a separate bowl, then add to the buttermilk mixture and whisk just until combined (a couple of streaks of flour is okay).

2   To make the blueberry sauce, add the blueberries and syrup to a saucepan and cook over a medium heat for 5–8 minutes until the blueberries have released their juices and the sauce has thickened slightly.

3   To cook the pancakes, heat a non-stick frying pan (it's helpful if this is a heavy-based one) over a medium-low heat. Give it 5 minutes or so to heat up thoroughly. Dollop dessertspoonfuls of your pancake mix into the pan (keep them on the smaller side as they will spread) – the batter should very gently fizzle. Add two peach slices to the top of each pancake, then cook until they have puffed up a bit, bubbles have started to appear on their surface and the undersides have turned golden, around 5–8 minutes. Gently flip the pancakes over with a wide spatula and cook on the second side for another minute, adding an extra teaspoon of ghee to help caramelise the peaches.

4   Remove the pancakes from the pan and stack them up to serve (or they can be kept warm in a low oven if you're cooking for many).

Tip American-style, leavened pancakes are best cooked low 'n' slow to ensure they turn out tall and fluffy.

whipped
salted yoghurt
with rooibos
peaches

These peaches have myriad
other uses: atop yoghurt
(for breakfast, rather than dessert),
or alongside cake – so do
consider doubling them.

balancing elements
yoghurt (sour/tangy)
rooibos (subtly bitter)
salt

*A dessert for people who don't really 'do' desserts: no baking required,
no complicated assembly – just a slightly tangy, slightly salty whipped
yoghurt with fragrant peaches poached in earthy rooibos. A light way
to end a summer meal.*

Serves 4

for the rooibos peaches
300ml (10fl oz/1⅓ cups) water
250g (9oz/1¼ cups) caster (superfine)
   or granulated sugar
5 rooibos teabags
4 cloves
¼ tsp fine sea salt
4 peaches, halved and pitted

for the whipped yoghurt
250g (9oz/1 cup plus 2 tbsp)
   thick Greek yoghurt (or labneh),
   fridge-cold
130g (4½oz/generous ½ cup)
   mascarpone, fridge-cold
1 tbsp runny honey
½ tsp flaky sea salt, plus extra
   to serve
120ml (4fl oz/½ cup) double (heavy)
   cream, fridge-cold

1   To poach the peaches, add all the ingredients except the fruit to
    a medium saucepan. Bring to the boil, stirring every so often, then turn
    the heat down to a bare simmer and add the peaches. Poach the fruit,
    flipping over halfway through, until soft and yielding (they'll also start
    to shed their skins), around 15–20 minutes. Once cooked, turn the heat
    off under the pan and leave the fruit to cool in the poaching liquid.
    Once cooled, you can remove the skins if you like.

2   Make the whipped yoghurt just before serving, as it is best cold. Whisk
    together the yoghurt, mascarpone, honey and salt. Separately, whisk the
    cream to soft peaks, then fold this through the yoghurt mix. Serve the
    whipped yoghurt in bowls along with the poached peaches. You can
    garnish the peaches with a couple of extra flakes of sea salt, if liked.

peach melba galette

When you want something quick and easy, this works perfectly well with store-bought puff pastry – simply halve the filling quantity.

Having said that, I do recommend making the pie dough if you have the time. It does require several hours to chill in the fridge, so I typically find it easiest to make a day or two in advance.

balancing element
raspberry (sour/tart)

In this life, most things are uncertain: What exists beyond this universe? Where will I be in ten years' time? Does he like me like that? But what is not in doubt is that a galette is one of the finest desserts there is. All the comfort of a pie, with none of the faff. Fruit-forward and therefore the perfect showcase for seasonal fruit. Effortless and therefore simultaneously cool and elegant. I am, and will always be, a big fan.

This one is a twist on Peach Melba, the dessert created by Escoffier for the Australian opera singer Dame Nellie Melba, with a hot peach and raspberry filling contrasted by cool, creamy vanilla ice cream.

Serves 8

300g (10½oz) fresh peaches, pitted and thinly sliced
juice of ½ lemon
3 tbsp caster (superfine) sugar
1½ tbsp cornflour (cornstarch)
pinch of fine sea salt
1 quantity of Pie Dough (see page 228)
100g (3½oz) fresh (or frozen) raspberries
1 tbsp whole milk
1 tbsp demerara (turbinado) sugar
vanilla ice cream, to serve

1 Preheat the oven to 170°C fan/190°C/375°F/gas 5.

2 Add the peaches to a bowl and squeeze over the lemon juice. Separately, whisk together the sugar, cornflour and salt, then add this to the peaches and gently toss everything together.

3 Roll out the pastry to 4mm (¼in) thick, then cut out a circle, around 30cm (12in) in diameter. Arrange the peach slices in the middle of the pastry disc, leaving a 3cm (1in) border around the edge, then scatter over the raspberries. Fold the pastry in over the fruit all the way around. Brush the pastry edges with milk, then sprinkle with the demerara sugar.

4 Bake until deeply golden, around 50 minutes, then allow to cool for 10 minutes before serving each slice with a ball of ice cream.

Tip When it comes to baking with pie dough (or puff pastry): it always needs longer in the oven than you think (see also the Pear + ACV Tarte Tatin on page 182). You'll be tempted to remove this galette halfway through the cooking time, but you'll be rewarded if you hold out. Keep an eye on it in the last 15 minutes of baking, and turn the oven down if it's getting too dark or the filling seems to be drying out.

boozy
baked
peaches

A particularly good recipe for sub-par peaches!

A high-quality ricotta (e.g. Seirass) will take this dessert from good to great – alternatively, whipped double (heavy) cream works wonderfully.

The amaretti in this dessert ensure that it is gluten free.

This can also be cooked on a barbecue (and is easily scaled up) – simply reduce the cooking time to account for the fiercer heat.

balancing elements
dark rum (subtly bitter)
light muscovado (subtle acidity)

Sometimes simple (and boozy) is best. Don't be suspicious of the short ingredient list: hot drunken peaches . . . soft, cooling whipped ricotta . . . the crunch of amaretti . . . you truly could not ask for anything more. The peach is given room to shine in this simpler version of the Piedmontese pesche ripiene (stuffed peaches).

Serves 2

for the peaches
2 peaches, halved and pitted
1 tbsp butter
1 tbsp light muscovado
    (or light brown) sugar
4 tbsp rum (or amaretto or bourbon)

for the amaretti cream
150g (5oz/⅔ cup) ricotta
    (or double/heavy cream)
1½ tsp honey
milk, to loosen (optional)
2 amaretti biscuits, crushed, plus
    extra to serve

1   Preheat the oven to 170°C fan/190°C/375°F/gas 5.

2   Get two sheets of kitchen foil and place two peach halves in the middle of each. Dot over little nuggets of butter, then sprinkle over the brown sugar. Gather the sides of the foil up to form a parcel around the peaches, add the rum and then close up completely. Place on a baking tray and bake for 30 minutes. Allow them to sit for around 10 minutes once out of the oven (not only to save you burning your tongue but also so that the peaches can wallow in the boozy juices).

3   While the peaches are cooling, whip together the ricotta and honey, adding milk to loosen if needed. Next, fold through the crushed amaretti.

4   To serve, add a couple of peach halves to each bowl, spoon over any remaining syrup from the bottom of the parcel, add a dollop of the amaretti cream, then crumble some more amaretti on top. Serve immediately.

peach, honey + ginger iced tea

The cold brew takes several hours, so do factor this in (I find it easiest to leave overnight).

If you can source loose-leaf sencha tea, that is ideal; however, tea bags also work here, as do other forms of green tea.

balancing elements
green tea (bitter)
lime (sour)
ginger (hot, subtly bitter)

Makes around 1.3 litres (2¼ pints)

for the tea
10g (¼oz) sencha tea
   (ideally loose leaf)
800ml (27fl oz/3⅓ cups)
   filtered water

for the peach syrup
450–500g (1lb–1lb 2oz)
   peaches, halved and pitted
500ml (17fl oz/generous
   2 cups) water
125g (4½oz/½ cup plus 2 tbsp) caster
   (superfine) or granulated sugar

for the lime + ginger syrup
100ml (3½fl oz/generous ⅓ cup)
   fresh lime juice
100g (3½oz/½ cup) caster (superfine)
   sugar
5cm (2in) piece of fresh root
   ginger, grated

to serve
juice of ½ lemon, or to taste
ice

This gorgeous, pink-hued iced tea makes the perfect drink for a summer lunch or picnic. Adapted from a recipe by Nicola Lamb, the ginger adds an additional fiery flavour kick.

1 Combine the tea and water and leave for a minimum of 6 hours (or overnight). After this time, strain the tea a couple of times through a fine sieve or muslin (cheesecloth).

2 To make the peach syrup, combine the ingredients in a medium saucepan and bring to a simmer. Cook gently for around 15 minutes, then turn off the heat and allow the peach halves to cool in the syrup.

3 For the lime and ginger syrup, stir together the ingredients in a small saucepan, bring to a simmer and cook for around 10 minutes until syrupy. Strain out the ginger and leave to cool completely.

4 To make the iced tea, combine the cold brew with half of the peach syrup (the peaches and remaining syrup can be stored in the fridge and eaten with yoghurt or porridge for breakfast, or ice cream for dessert) and the lime and ginger syrup. Add more peach syrup (I usually add two-thirds of the the peach syrup in total) and lemon juice to taste, then serve over ice.

tipsy white peach + basil granita

This granita will need several hours in the freezer – and due to the alcohol content it won't freeze super hard.

The perfect summer dessert when hosting anyone who is gluten- or dairy-free.

balancing elements
rosé wine (subtly acidic/bitter)
lemon juice (sour)
basil (herbal)

I've made no secret of my love of granita – something I previously thought was unlikely to be all that exciting but have come to realise is quite special. This one screams summer, with its seasonal peaches, basil and a decent glug of rosé. Any lover of Italian cuisine will recognise the inspiration: that romantic Italian tradition of eating peaches that have been sitting in wine.

**Serves 4 as a dessert,
or 8-10 as a palate cleanser**

300ml (10fl oz/1¼ cups) rosé wine
200ml (7fl oz/generous ¾ cup) water
125g (4½oz/½ cup plus 2 tbsp) caster (superfine) sugar
6 firm but ripe white peaches, halved and pitted
6 basil leaves
juice of ½–1 lemon, to taste

1   Place a small, lipped metal tray (or similar) in the freezer to chill.

2   Combine the wine, water and sugar in a saucepan and bring to the boil, stirring occasionally to ensure that the sugar has dissolved. Add the peach halves and basil, then turn the heat down slightly and simmer for around 15 minutes. Fish out the peaches (these can be eaten with yoghurt for breakfast) and measure your liquid – you should have 500–600ml (17fl oz–1 pint/generous 2–2½ cups). Add the lemon juice to taste, then allow to cool completely.

3   Pour the syrup into the chilled tray and place back in the freezer for around 2 hours.

4   After this time, run a fork through the mix to break up any ice that has started to form, then return it to the freezer. Repeat this twice more until you have a mound of soft, pale pink ice crystals. Serve unadorned.

coconut

To travel around Sri Lanka – along its coasts, through its hilly central area (where all the Ceylon tea is grown), and up to the Tamil region in the north – is to travel across a land of coconuts. Coconut palms line your path, and the many products derived from this single type of tree are woven into the fabric of Sri Lankan life. Fresh coconut milk graces curries, coconut oil is used for frying, and coconut vinegar adds piquancy to pickles, such as *brinjal moju* (sweet and sour aubergine). The sap of the unopened coconut flower is boiled to produce *kithul* (Sri Lankan 'maple syrup'), and reduced further to produce *kithul jaggery*, a form of palm sugar. Coconut water replenishes electrolytes lost in the tropical heat, while coconut wine and *arrack* (a coconut-based spirit) encourage relaxation and socialising. Coconut shells, meanwhile, become kitchen utensils, or charcoal, or line pathways, or polish floors. What can't the coconut do?

Sitting at home, it's clear that the coconut – a token of holidays and cocktails here in London – is a symbol of life in the countries in which it grows (including Indonesia, parts of India, the Philippines, Brazil, Vietnam and the Caribbean). Diana Lutz put it most succinctly: '(The coconut is) the Swiss Army knife of the plant kingdom' – and it is perhaps for this reason that it has come to mean so much to so many. To Hindus, coconuts are divine ('God's fruit' in Sanskrit): they symbolise luck and prosperity, they welcome Lakshmi, goddess of wealth, and they are a common offering in temples and Hindu ceremonies. Meanwhile, fisherman in India will offer coconuts to the seas in hopes of a bountiful catch.

It's fair to say that coconut is one of the most versatile ingredients, used widely in both savoury and sweet dishes. Fresh coconut is mild, milky and gently sweet, but once dried and toasted it becomes more assertive, tending to divide the crowd. I am a firm fan (Bounty is my favourite chocolate in the Celebrations box) but, in my experience, while it is tolerated well enough in savoury dishes, many struggle with it in sweet contexts. This makes sense because coconut is already sweet and rich, so adding sugar and more richness (from butter, eggs, etc.) can result in something cloying, both in flavour and mouthfeel. For this reason, coconut loves sharp, tangy or bitter flavours such as passionfruit (see page 118), lime (page 127), raspberries (page 116) and dark chocolate (page 122), since they offer essential balance.

Coconut is available in many forms in the supermarket, perhaps most commonly as tins of coconut milk, perfect for curries or soups. These will often separate into a more watery liquid and a thicker, richer cream – essentially coconut water and coconut cream – so are worth a shake before you use. You can buy both coconut water and coconut cream as separate products, but it's important to note that coconut cream and *creamed* coconut are not the same: where the former is a thick cream, the latter is a solid block that can be broken up and melted or turned into a form of coconut cream/milk by adding boiled water (useful if you are cooking for just one or two). Coconut oil – which can be milder and more highly processed, or cold-pressed and stronger in coconut flavour – is ideal for cooking many southeast Asian dishes, but I also love it when making granola (page 115) or in the biscuit base of a cheesecake, especially where more tropical flavours are involved (see the Piña Colada Cheesecake on page 127).

When it comes to the baking cupboard, you can buy dried coconut in various forms: desiccated (which you can rehydrate) and flaked (often decorative, sometimes sweetened). Sweetened coconut condensed milk is also available – a useful ingredient for desserts such as Key lime pie, cheesecake or ice creams. In fact, coconut products are incredibly useful when it comes to vegan baking and desserts, adding richness and creaminess without the need for butter (see the Vegan Coconut + Lime Loaf on page 125). You'll also find the coconut spirit Malibu in the supermarkets, of course, lending a tropical twist to many a cocktail. Just as coconuts can be found all over Sri Lanka, and other tropical climates, their products – albeit rarely in any sort of fresh form – seem to have become surprisingly prolific in temperate climates too.

laura's coconut-filled pancakes (sri lankan pani pol)

It's best (but not essential) to give the crêpe batter 30 minutes to rest.

These crêpes can keep for a few days in the fridge, but are best brought back up to room temperature before eating.

balancing elements
cardamom (subtly bitter)
turmeric (bitter)
jaggery (subtly sour)
clove (herbal, bitter)

This recipe, shared with me by my friend Laura Hicks (a fellow MasterChef contestant with Sri Lankan heritage), comes from a book that's been in her family for almost 100 years. Made up of Sri Lankan recipes written by the hands of Laura's great-grandmother, grandmother, mother and aunties (you can catch a glimpse of it on her Instagram @lauraspicekitchen), it's a precious symbol of her family history.

I first tried these slightly spongy, turmeric-tinged crêpes rolled around a sweet, cardamom-scented coconut filling a few years ago when in Sri Lanka and immediately fell in love. If you have a sweet tooth, then these are for you, although the cardamom and spices help balance the sweetness. Laura's grandmother remembers a delivery man, nicknamed 'the chunpun man', who used to travel on a rickshaw around the local villages at around 4pm every day, selling pani pol (along with other treats). He would always blast the same song so that people would know it was him. Needless to say, these make the perfect afternoon sweet treat.

Makes around 6–8

2 eggs
150ml (5fl oz/⅔ cup) whole milk
80ml (3fl oz/⅓ cup) water
60ml (2½fl oz/¼ cup) vegetable oil
1 tbsp kithul treacle
    (or maple syrup)
½ tsp vanilla bean paste
    or extract
100g (3½oz/generous ¾ cup)
    plain (all-purpose) flour
¼ tsp baking powder
¼ tsp ground turmeric

for the coconut filling
100g (3½oz/½ cup) jaggery
    (or dark muscovado sugar)
4 tsp water
½ cinnamon stick
3 cardamom pods, seeds removed
    and ground (or ¾ tsp ground
    cardamom)
1 clove
300g (10½oz/5 cups) freshly grated
    coconut (or desiccated/
    unsweetened shredded coconut)

equipment
blender (helpful, not essential)
20cm (8in) frying pan (skillet)

1   To make the crêpe batter, add the wet ingredients to a blender and briefly blitz, before adding the dry ingredients. Blend just until the batter is smooth and without lumps, no longer. Set aside to rest for at least 30 minutes.

2   For the filling, combine the sugar, water, cinnamon, cardamom and clove in a medium saucepan and set over a low heat. Once the sugar has melted, turn the heat up to medium. Just before the mixture starts to boil, fold in the coconut and turn the heat back down slightly. If the mixture is too moist, continue to cook until all the sugar has been soaked up by the coconut and the mixture is sticky and firm.

3   To cook the crêpes, heat your pan over a medium-high heat, then pour a ladle of batter into the pan, swirling to cover the surface evenly (we're going for slightly thicker, spongier crêpes here rather than thin ones, so that they can fold without cracking). You want the pan to be hot enough that the batter will create little bubbles on the surface. Cook on each side for around 20 seconds, until the crêpe is lightly golden. Remove to a waiting plate and repeat with the rest of the batter.

4   To assemble, place a couple of tablespoons of the coconut mixture to one side of a crêpe. Fold over the sides of the crêpe to the centre, then roll to form a log shape. Repeat with the rest of the crêpes (you may have a little filling left over – chef's treat! Or it can be frozen).

Tip Most batters – whether for Yorkshire puddings, crêpes, blinis, farinata, etc. – benefit from some resting time before cooking, as this allows the flour to properly absorb the liquid. See also Crêpes with Plantain + Rum Caramel (page 68), Russian Honey (Crêpe) Cake (page 168) and Currant Dutch Baby with Honeyed Ricotta (page 192).

jamaican cornmeal porridge

This is easily made vegan: simply substitute the condensed milk for a vegan version (Carnation do one) and serve with a plant-based milk of choice (I like coconut or cashew m*lk).

balancing elements
bay leaf (herbal/aniseed)
light muscovado (subtle acidity)

Serves 2–3

400ml (14fl oz/1⅔ cups) water
1 x 400ml (14fl oz) tin of coconut milk
1 bay leaf, torn in half
¼ tsp fine sea salt
90g (3¼oz/generous ¾ cup) fine cornmeal (I use Dunn's River)
75g (3oz/¼ cup) condensed milk
1 tsp vanilla bean paste
1–2 tbsp light muscovado (or soft light brown) sugar, to taste
milk, to serve
nutmeg, for grating

Jamaican cornmeal porridge is a delicious way to rise 'n' shine, offering sweet, gentle comfort. Jamaicans call this breakfast, but I confess that I like it just as much for pudding.

1   Add the water, coconut milk, bay leaf and salt to a pan and cook over a medium-high heat until steaming.

2   Slowly pour a stream of cornmeal into the liquid, whisking as you go. Once the cornmeal has been incorporated, turn the heat down to its lowest setting and cook gently, whisking frequently, until the cornmeal has thickened and cooked through, around 5–10 minutes.

3   Remove the bay leaf, then whisk in the condensed milk and vanilla. Add sugar to taste, then serve immediately in bowls, adding a small moat of milk to each and grating over some fresh nutmeg.

double coconut granola

To make a chocolate version of this granola, add 2 tablespoons cocoa powder to the dry ingredients, melt 150g (5oz) dark chocolate into the warm coconut oil and bake the granola at 130°C fan/150°C/300°F/gas 2 for 40–45 minutes.

balancing elements
cardamom (subtly bitter),
dark chocolate (if using – bitter)
salt

Few things feel more wholesome (and doable!) than making a homemade batch of granola. The pros are many: it's low effort, makes several days' worth of breakfasts, is considerably healthier than store-bought stuff and, well, most importantly, it's delicious. Though you can ring the changes when it comes to the fat used (olive oil is popular), I find coconut oil to be the gold standard for granola as it contributes sweetness without additional sugar. And while this is a double coconut situation – with both coconut oil and coconut flakes making an appearance – it isn't strongly coconutty, just really very tasty.

Makes 8–10 servings

300g (10½oz/3 cups) rolled oats
120g (4½oz) flaked coconut
120g (4½oz) pumpkin seeds
60g (2¼oz) sunflower seeds
1 tsp ground cardamom
½ tsp fine sea salt
120ml (4fl oz/½ cup) extra-virgin
   coconut oil
120ml (4fl oz/½ cup) maple syrup

1 Preheat the oven to 140°C fan/160°C/325°F/gas 3 and line your baking trays with greaseproof paper (or silicone baking mats).

2 Stir together all the dry ingredients in a large bowl.

3 Separately, melt the coconut oil in a small pan over a low heat. Remove from the heat and add the maple syrup.

4 Pour the coconut oil and maple syrup mixture into the dry ingredients and stir until evenly damp.

5 Spread the granola over the baking trays in a thin, even layer and bake until golden and crisp, around 35–40 minutes (I switch the baking trays around hallway through this time, and stir the granola too, to ensure even cooking). Allow to cool completely before transferring to an airtight container.

Tip For big cluster granola (and some extra protein!) stir through an egg white that has been briefly whipped until frothy. Then when baking avoid stirring! Instead use a spatula to turn over sections of the granola carefully, to minimise breaking them up.

raspberry + coconut hand pies

The pie dough requires several hours of chilling in the fridge – I find it easiest to make it a day or two in advance.

The pie dough makes these knockout, but for a speedier bake, you could make these with store-bought puff pastry instead (you may not get exactly the same number of pies).

balancing elements
raspberries (sour, tart)
pie dough (salty, flaky)
light muscovado (subtle acidity)

I don't know about you, but no matter how much I love a fruit Danish, the process of making them (i.e. yeasted dough, elaborate folds and precise timings) ensures that I'm never going to try them at home – they sit firmly in the category of things that I am happy to pay someone else to make for me. Hand pies/turnovers, on the other hand, involve about as much time and effort as I'm prepared to put into something that is guaranteed to disappear pretty quickly in my house. Truthfully, they're almost no effort if you opt for store-bought puff pastry (although I would urge you to make the pie dough if you can). These hand pies are inspired by Bajan coconut turnovers, but the addition of raspberries adds what I would consider essential moisture, plus a bright pop of tartness.

Makes 6–7

for the filling
75g (3oz/1 cup)
    desiccated (unsweetened
    shredded) coconut
½ tsp ground allspice
½ tsp ground cinnamon
½ tsp mixed spice
generous pinch of fine sea salt
50g (2oz) butter
40g (1½oz/3 tbsp)
    light muscovado
    (or light brown) sugar
120g (4½oz) raspberries,
    fresh or frozen

to assemble
1 quantity of Pie Dough
    (see page 228)
plain (all-purpose) flour, for dusting
1 egg, whisked, for sealing
demerara (turbinado) sugar,
    for sprinkling

1   Combine the coconut, spices and salt in a bowl. Separately, add the butter and sugar to a small saucepan and place over a medium heat, stirring occasionally until melted. Take off the heat, stir in the spiced coconut mixture until evenly combined, then lightly fold through the raspberries until the mix is slightly marbled. Set aside to cool completely (it's important that the filling isn't hot when you make the turnovers, otherwise the residual heat will melt the butter in the pastry).

2   On a well-floured surface, roll out the pie dough to a large square, 3mm (⅛in) thick. Cut the pastry into discs using a 10cm (4in) cutter (you need an even number of discs – you should get about 12–14). Brush the edges of each disc with egg wash. Add 2 tablespoons of filling into the centre of half of the discs, then place the remaining discs on top. Press the edges together, then seal with the tines of a fork. Transfer the parcels to a lined baking tray and place in the fridge to chill for 30 minutes.

3   Preheat the oven to 200°C fan/220°C/425°F/gas 7.

4   Brush the hand pies with egg wash and use a small knife to create a couple of slits in the top of each pie. Sprinkle each with ½ teaspoon of demerara sugar. Place in the oven and immediately turn the heat down to 180°C fan/200°C/400°F/gas 6. Bake until deeply golden and the bases are cooked, around 20–25 minutes.

5   Leave to cool for 10 minutes before serving warm with ice cream (or they are also delicious eaten plain at room temperature).

Tip When it comes to baking with pie dough (or puff pastry): it always needs a lot longer in the oven than you think (see also the Pear + ACV Tarte Tatin on page 182, or Black Tea Eccles Cakes on page 198). You'll be tempted to remove these hand pies after 10–15 minutes, because they'll look golden, but you'll be rewarded if you hold out. If you are worried about them getting too brown, simply turn the oven down to 160°C fan/180°C/350°F/gas 4.

coconut cream pie with passionfruit

A number of the elements require some time in the fridge, so I find it easiest to make the pastry and curd in advance. The sweet pastry (page 229) can be made couple of days ahead and the passionfruit curd can be made up to 5 days ahead and stored in the fridge. The coconut custard can also be made a day in advance.

To make this a quicker bake, you could buy a ready-made pastry case (bear in mind that this might be shallower than a homemade case, so you may end up with some extra filling), as well as sweetened coconut flakes (I like Urban Fruit).

Avoid using rich-yolk eggs for the custard – they give a disconcertingly pink hue.

balancing elements
passionfruit (sour)
lemon juice (sour)
salt

Is it a cream pie? Is it a tart? Truthfully, I'm still not sure. Is it delicious? Undoubtedly. Luscious, gently sweet coconut custard, topped with toasty coconut flakes, is kept in check by a sharp, assertive passionfruit curd. I feel that I ought to let you know that this tastes and slices best on day two, but – really – good luck holding out that long.

The passionfruit curd is adapted from a recipe by Nigella.

Serves 8

for the coconut custard
1 litre (1¾ pints/4 cups) whole milk
100g (3½oz/½ cup) caster (superfine) sugar
125g (4½oz/1⅔ cups) desiccated (unsweetened shredded) coconut
60g (2½oz/½ cup) cornflour (cornstarch)
¼ tsp fine salt
2 eggs
3 egg yolks
15g (½oz) butter

for the curd
5 passionfruit
1 egg
1 egg yolk
70g (2¼oz/scant ⅓ cup) caster (superfine) sugar
45g (1¾oz) butter
fresh lemon juice, to taste

1   Start with the coconut custard. In a medium saucepan, heat the milk with 60g (2½oz/generous ¼ cup) of the sugar and the desiccated coconut until the milk just begins to simmer. Remove from the heat and leave to infuse for 30 minutes. Strain through a sieve (pressing to ensure you squeeze out all the milk), then return the milk to the saucepan and discard the coconut. Gently reheat the milk until it's steaming, then take off the heat.

2   In a medium bowl, whisk together the remaining sugar, cornflour, salt, eggs and yolks until lightened in colour, around 1 minute. Pour a third of the warmed coconut-flavoured milk into the eggs, then whisk this mixture into the milk in the pan over a medium-low heat. Whisk constantly until the mixture begins to thicken, around 5–10 minutes (it'll stay the same for a while, but when it turns, it turns quickly). Once it starts to thicken, whisk for another minute, getting into all the corners of the pan. Take off the heat and whisk in the butter. Transfer to a container, cover the surface with cling film (plastic wrap), and refrigerate until chilled, around 3 hours.

3   For the passionfruit curd, remove the pulp from the passionfruit, place in the blender and blitz for a second or two to loosen the seeds, then strain. In a small bowl, whisk together the egg, yolk and sugar. Separately, melt the butter over a low heat in a medium saucepan, then stir in the egg mixture and strained passionfruit juice. Keep cooking gently, stirring constantly, and turning the heat up slightly if required, until thickened. Transfer to a jar or container, allow to cool slightly, then transfer to the fridge for at least 2 hours. Once cooled, I might add fresh lemon juice to taste – especially if my passionfruit were on the sweeter side.

for the tart case

1 quantity of Sweet Pastry
  (see page 229)
  (or a ready-made tart case)
1 egg white, beaten, for sealing
  the pastry case

for the coconut flakes

50g (2oz/1 cup) dried coconut flakes
1½ tbsp maple syrup
¼ tsp flaky sea salt
icing (confectioners') sugar,
  to serve (optional)

equipment

blender (e.g. Nutribullet) or small
  bowl of a food processor
23cm (9in) loose-bottomed tart tin,
  sides 3–4cm (1–1½in) high

4 Meanwhile, prepare your tart case. Take the pastry out of the fridge and allow to warm up slightly on the side, around 30 minutes. Roll the pastry out on a well-floured surface until it's slightly thicker than a pound coin (and large enough for your tart tin), around 4–5mm (½in) thick (you want to err on the thicker side with this, so that it can hold the custard filling). The trick to this is taking your time (don't roll out the pastry too aggressively, use light pressure) and making sure everything is well floured. Gently roll the pastry around your rolling pin, then drape over the tart tin. Use your fingers (or a small ball of pastry dough) to gently tease/press the pastry into the corners. Fix any breaks with spare scraps of excess pastry. Trim the edges using a small knife at a 45° angle away from the tin and prick the base with a fork (to prevent air bubbles). Transfer to the fridge to chill for at least 40 minutes.

5 Around 10–15 minutes before you plan on removing the tart case from the fridge, preheat the oven to 180°C fan/200°C/400°F/gas 6.

6 Remove the pastry case from the fridge and line with kitchen foil and ceramic baking beans (or dried pulses). Place in the oven and immediately turn the heat down to 160°C fan/180°C/350°F/gas 4. Bake until the edges are lightly golden, around 15 minutes, then gently remove the baking beans and foil. Brush the base of the tart with the beaten egg white and return to the oven until firm and solidly golden, another 7–10 minutes. (This case won't get baked any further so you're looking for the pastry to be completely cooked, as opposed to just blind baked.) Allow to cool completely.

7 Meanwhile, line a baking tray with greaseproof paper. Combine the ingredients for the coconut flakes and space them out over the tray. Bake until lightly golden, around 5 minutes (check regularly once they've had the first 3 minutes). Allow to cool completely.

8 To assemble the tart, briefly whisk the coconut custard until smooth, then dollop spoonfuls across the tart case. Use a spatula or the back of a spoon to gently level the top. The tart can be stored in the fridge at this point. To serve, scatter the coconut flakes on top and dust with a little icing sugar. Serve the passionfruit curd alongside.

chocolate 'dream' cake (danish drømmekage)

balancing elements
light muscovado (subtle acidity)
dark chocolate (bitter)
cocoa powder (bitter)
buttermilk (sour/tangy)
salt

Makes 15 large squares (or 24 smaller ones)

120g (4½oz) butter, melted
75g (3oz) dark chocolate (70% cocoa solids), roughly chopped
150ml (5fl oz/⅔ cup) buttermilk
¼ tsp fine sea salt
130g (4½oz/1 cup) plain (all-purpose) flour
75g (3oz/¾ cup) cocoa powder
20g (¾oz/1 tbsp plus 2 tsp) cornflour (cornstarch)
2 tsp baking powder
¼ tsp bicarbonate of soda (baking soda)
3 eggs, at room temperature
250g (9oz/1¼ cups) caster (superfine) sugar

for the topping
200g (7oz/3 cups) desiccated (unsweetened shredded) coconut
150g (5oz) butter
150g (5oz/¾ cup) light muscovado (or light brown) sugar
100g (3½oz/¼ cup) golden syrup
2 tsp vanilla bean paste
¾ tsp fine sea salt

equipment
20 x 30cm (8 x 12in) traybake tin
electric hand whisk
kitchen blowtorch (helpful, not essential)

Soft, plain sponge topped with a crispy-chewy mixture of coconut and brown sugar that caramelises on top: a dream. And with the added bitterness of dark chocolate to the cake batter, this is a gently chocolatey version of that dream.

1 Preheat the oven to 160°C fan/180°C/350°F/gas 4. Line the cake tin with greaseproof paper.

2 Melt together the butter and chocolate over a very low heat, then combine with the buttermilk and salt. Separately, whisk together the flour, cocoa, cornflour, baking powder and bicarb in a bowl.

3 Using an electric hand whisk, whip up the eggs and caster sugar together until pale, doubled in volume and at ribbon stage – this may take as long as 10 minutes.

4 Gently fold half of the melted butter mixture into the egg mixture, then sift in half of the flour mix, taking care not to knock the air out. Repeat. Pour into the tin and place this onto a baking tray, then transfer to the oven. Bake until evenly risen and the cake springs back when you touch it, around 15 minutes.

5 While the cake is baking, make the topping. Start by adding the coconut to a dry medium saucepan and toast until golden, stirring every so often to ensure it's evenly browned. Transfer to a bowl, wipe out the pan, then add the butter, sugar, golden syrup, vanilla and salt. Place over a medium-low heat until the butter and sugar are melted and glossy (you want the sugar to have fully dissolved). Increase the heat to medium-high and simmer until thickened, around 5 minutes. Stir through the coconut and remove from the heat.

6 As soon as the cake comes out of the oven, turn it up to 200°C fan/ 220°C/425°F/gas 7. Pour the coconut topping over the top of the cake and use an offset spatula or back of a spoon to spread it evenly over the surface. Return the cake to the oven and bake until the top is turning golden, around 5–10 minutes. Once out of the oven you can use a blowtorch to get a bit of additional colour across the top, if you like. Allow to cool fully before slicing into squares (a serrated bread knife will ensure the cleanest cut).

Tip To make 'faux' buttermilk, simply combine 250ml (8½fl oz/generous 1 cup) whole milk with 5 tablespoons fresh lemon juice. See also: Strawberry + Cream Cake (page 76), Date, Fennel Seed + Lemon Scones (page 200).

coconut

toasted anzac biscuits

ANZAC biscuits are quick and easy to make, and perfect for gifting as they'll keep in an airtight container for at least a couple of weeks.

balancing elements
brown butter (subtle umami)
ground ginger (hot/fiery)
salt

There may be no better biscuit than the Australian ANZAC biscuit (think flapjack in cookie form). Caramelised, chewy and subtly coconutty, if you're able to stop at one, well, then you're a stronger person than I. Adapted from a recipe shared with me by my best friend Katie (whose mum is Australian), neither browning the butter nor the addition of ground ginger are traditional but I love the toasty, subtly spicy notes that both offer, especially around Christmas.

Makes around 14 biscuits

2 tbsp boiled water
¼ tsp bicarbonate of soda (baking soda)
180g (6oz) butter
40g (1½oz/scant 2 tbsp) golden syrup
90g (3¼oz/1¼ cups) desiccated (unsweetened shredded) coconut
120g (4½oz/1 cup) plain (all-purpose) flour
90g (3¼oz/1 cup) rolled oats
130g (4½oz/generous ⅔ cup) muscovado (or light brown) sugar
90g (3¼oz/scant ½ cup) granulated sugar
1½ tsp ground ginger
¼ tsp fine sea salt

equipment
2–3 of your largest baking trays
large round cookie cutter, for 'scooting' (helpful, not essential)

1   Preheat the oven to 160°C fan/180°C/350°F/gas 4. Line your baking trays with a silicone baking mat (or greaseproof paper). If you only have one tray, simply bake the biscuits in batches.

2   Stir together the boiled water and bicarb.

3   In a small saucepan, brown the butter over a medium heat, taking it as far as you can without burning it – this will take around 5–10 minutes. Strain out the toasted milk solids using a piece of muslin or a very fine strainer, then stir in the golden syrup and water-bicarb mixture until melted. Set aside.

4   Meanwhile, in a frying pan (skillet), toast the desiccated coconut until golden. Allow to cool for a minute or two, then combine with the flour, oats, sugars, ginger and salt.

5   Pour the butter-golden syrup mixture into the dry ingredients and stir until combined (word of advice: try not to eat too much of the raw biscuit dough at this point). If you like, you can chill the mix to help minimise the spread of the cookies. Otherwise, go straight ahead and roll the dough into balls the size of gobstoppers, then place on the lined baking tray(s), leaving plenty of space between them (4–6 per tray).

6   Bake until they have spread out and have turned golden brown around the edges, around 14 minutes. For perfectly round biscuits, as soon as they are out of the oven take the cookie cutter, place it around each biscuit in turn, gently moving it in a circular motion to nudge them into a rounded shape (this is called 'scooting') – I find it best to take one tray out of the oven, quickly scoot the cookies, and then take the next tray out and repeat (this ensures that the cookies don't set before you have time to scoot them).

7   Transfer the cookies to a wire rack to cool and firm up for 5 minutes or so. I like to eat them when they're still a bit warm but they also keep well for a couple of weeks in an airtight container.

vegan coconut + lime loaf

The texture of the cake is best on the day of baking.

balancing elements
lime juice (sour)
lime zest (subtly bitter)
olive oil (subtly bitter)

While I find it easy enough to create 'casually vegan' dishes in the world of savoury food, it's considerably harder to craft legitimately delicious vegan desserts. Which is why I'm so delighted to present you with this cake, adapted from a recipe by Posie Brien. Vegan cakes can be a little cloying, due to the absence of eggs, but the sharpness of lime offers brightness of flavour here, while the coconut ensures a rich, moist crumb.

Makes around 8–10 slices

zest and juice of 2 limes
150g (5oz/¾ cup) caster (superfine) or granulated sugar
200ml (7fl oz/generous ¾ cup) unsweetened almond milk (or other non-dairy milk)
45ml (3 tbsp) olive oil
1 tsp vanilla bean paste
180g (6oz/scant 1½ cups) plain (all-purpose) flour
1 tsp baking powder
½ tsp bicarbonate of soda (baking soda)
¼ tsp fine sea salt
½ tsp ground cinnamon
50g (2oz/generous ½ cup) desiccated (unsweetened shredded) coconut, lightly toasted

for the icing
75g (3oz/¾ cup) icing (confectioners') sugar
juice of 1 lime

equipment
900g (2lb) loaf tin

1   Preheat the oven to 180°C fan/200°C/400°F/gas 6. Line your loaf tin (see tip).

2   In a large bowl, rub the lime zest into the sugar, then whisk in the lime juice, almond milk, olive oil and vanilla.

3   Separately, combine the flour, baking powder, bicarb, salt and cinnamon in a bowl. Stir the dry ingredients into the wet until just combined, then fold through the coconut.

4   Pour the batter into the prepared tin and bake until risen, golden on top and an inserted skewer comes out clean, around 30 minutes. Set aside to cool slightly before removing from the tin.

5   Once the cake has cooled completely, combine the icing sugar and half the lime juice, whisking until there are no lumps. Add the rest of the lime juice, a teaspoon at a time, until you have the right consistency of glaze, then pour this over the cake. If you like you can allow the glaze to fully set – or feel free to dig in immediately.

Tip Loaf tin liners are available in most major supermarkets and will make your baking life infinitely easier! See also: Simple Citrus, Olive Oil + Vanilla Loaf (page 142) and French Yoghurt Pot Loaf (page 160).

piña colada cheesecake

This requires an overnight stint in the fridge.

Philadelphia cream cheese is essential for cheesecakes as it is sufficiently stable.

When it comes to the pineapple topping, I use light muscovado sugar for the caramel notes it contributes, but for a brighter yellow colour switch this for caster (superfine) sugar.

balancing elements
cream cheese (sour/tangy)
sour cream (sour/tangy)
lime juice (sour)
lime zest (subtly bitter)
white rum (bitter)

Serves 8–10

for the base
50g (2oz) butter
40ml (1¾fl oz/1 tbsp plus 2 tsp) coconut oil
30g (1oz/2 tbsp) light muscovado (or soft light brown) sugar
generous pinch of fine sea salt
125g (4oz) Nice biscuits
125g (4oz) digestive biscuits
1 egg white (optional)

for the filling
3 x 165g (5½oz) packs of cream cheese, at room temperature
30g (1oz/2 heaped tbsp) caster (superfine) sugar
2 eggs
210g (7½oz/1 cup) sweetened condensed coconut milk (I use Biona)
150g (5oz/generous ½ cup) sour cream
zest and juice of 1 lime
10g (¼oz/1 tbsp) cornflour (cornstarch), sifted
½ tsp flaky sea salt

for the pineapple topping
½ large Bramley cooking apple
zest and juice of 1 lime
50ml (2fl oz/3 tbsp plus 1 tsp) white rum
½ tbsp cornflour (cornstarch)
300g (10½oz) pineapple, finely chopped (approx. ½ large pineapple)
50g (2oz/3½ tbsp) light muscovado (or soft light brown) sugar

equipment
20cm (8in) (or 23cm/9in) non-stick springform cake tin

A holiday in cheesecake form – need I say more?

1 Preheat the oven to 160°C fan/180°C/350°F/gas 4. Line the base of the tin with a circle of greaseproof paper.

2 For the biscuit base, melt the butter, coconut oil, brown sugar and salt in a small saucepan. Add the biscuits to a sealed plastic sandwich bag and roll over them with a rolling pin until a medium-coarse crumb is reached (you don't want powder). Stir the crushed biscuits into the melted mixture until combined and the texture is like damp sand. Add a third of the mixture to the cake tin and use your fingers to press it two-thirds of the way up the sides, then add the rest of the mixture and press it into the bottom of the tin. Use a flat-sided glass to pack everything in evenly. If you like, brush the base with some egg white, to help seal it.

3 Bake the biscuit base until lightly golden at the edges, 10–12 minutes, then set aside to cool.

4 In a large bowl, whisk the cream cheese for the filling until loosened, then whisk in the sugar until dissolved. Add the eggs, one at a time, beating well between each addition. Follow with the condensed coconut milk, sour cream, lime zest and juice. Pour a small amount of the mixture into a little bowl, sift over the cornflour, then add the salt. Whisk until this mixture has no lumps (you can add a little more of the cheesecake mix, if it's too thick/dry). Pour this mixture back into the large bowl, using a spatula to ensure you get every last bit. Whisk everything together until combined.

5 Pour the filling into the prepared base and bake until there's still a decent wiggle in the middle but the edges have set and the top is firm to touch, around 30 minutes. Turn the oven off and leave the cheesecake in there for 15 minutes before removing and allowing the cheesecake to cool completely. Transfer to the fridge to chill overnight (or for at least 4 hours).

6 To make the pineapple topping, peel and purée the Bramley apple, then combine it with the lime juice and half of the rum to stop the apple going brown. Next, whisk in the cornflour until there are no lumps. Transfer to a saucepan and stir through the pineapple and light muscovado sugar. Set over a medium-low heat and stir every so often until the sugar is melted, around 5 minutes. Increase the heat until the mixture is bubbling gently, then cook until thickened and the pineapple is starting to go translucent and a little glossy, another 15 minutes or so. Finally, stir in the rest of the rum and the lime zest, then allow to cool completely.

7 To serve, remove the cheesecake from the fridge around 30 minutes beforehand, release from the tin and top with the pineapple topping.

Tip Every cheesecake benefits from an overnight stint in the fridge, tempting though it is to eat it immediately – it's this step that ensures a luscious creamy texture. See also: Milky Bar Basque Cheesecake (page 136).

mango, coconut + lime layer cake

balancing elements
lime juice (sour)
lime zest (subtly bitter)
sour cream (sour/tangy)

Serves 10–12

for the mango + lime curd
150ml (5fl oz/⅔ cup) mango purée, fresh or tinned
70g (2¼oz/scant ⅓ cup) caster (superfine) sugar
juice of 1 large lime (around 2 tbsp)
1 egg, plus 1 egg yolk
1 tbsp cornflour (cornstarch)
pinch of fine sea salt
70g (2¼oz) butter, at room temperature, cubed

for the sponges
100g (3½oz/generous 1 cup) desiccated (unsweetened shredded) coconut
zest and juice of 3 limes
340g (11¾oz) butter, cubed
340g (11¾oz/1½ cups) caster (superfine) sugar
6 eggs
340g (11¾oz/2¾ cups) self-raising flour

for the lime syrup
juice of 3 limes (around 100ml/ 3½fl oz/generous ⅓ cup)
100g (3½oz/½ cup) caster (superfine) sugar

for the cream
300ml (10fl oz/1⅓ cups) double (heavy) cream, fridge-cold
25g (1oz/3 tbsp) icing (confectioners') sugar
300ml (10fl oz/1⅓ cups) sour cream

to decorate
2 tbsp shredded (or desiccated) coconut, lightly toasted

equipment
3 x 20cm (8in) non-stick sandwich cake tins, lined
electric hand whisk

My sandwich tins are on the taller side (5cm/2in) – if yours are more shallow then you may want to bake this in more than 3 layers (adjust the baking time down if this is the case).

The curd can be made up to 3 days ahead. Store in the fridge.

If you only have 2 tins, bake those first, then re-use one of the tins to bake the third layer.

This joyous, sunny cake is spectacular for birthdays, although I must qualify that it doesn't transport well since I've avoided buttercream (I know, I know – but we talked about this on page 9). The truth is that I prefer the combination of double (heavy) cream and sour cream for the filling as it offers a bit of tang (flavour over logistics, always). If you are wanting to take this to a birthday party, your best bet is to transport the elements (cakes, curd) separately, along with the ingredients for the cream filling, then whip that up and assemble on site.

1 To make the curd, place all the ingredients except the butter in a medium–large bowl set over a pan of gently simmering water. Stir until the sugar has dissolved, then whisk until the curd starts to thicken, around 10–15 minutes. Gradually whisk in the cubes of butter until melted and cook for a couple more minutes until thickened. Strain the curd through a fine sieve, then cover the surface with a piece of cling film (plastic wrap) and set aside to cool fully before transferring to the fridge.

2 Preheat the oven to 160°C fan/180°C/350°F/gas 4.

3 Cover the desiccated coconut for the sponges with the lime juice and set aside. Cream together the butter, sugar and lime zest until light and fluffy, the sugar has dissolved and the mixture is pale yellow – this will take a good 10 minutes. Whisk in the eggs, one at a time, blending thoroughly between each addition. Stir through the soaked coconut mix, then sift in the flour and gently fold through until combined.

4 Divide the batter evenly between the tins. Use an offset spatula (or back of a spoon) to level out the tops, then add a circle of greaseproof paper to the top of each (see tip). Bake until a skewer comes out clean, around 18–22 minutes. Cool for 5–10 minutes before turning out of the tins.

5 Meanwhile, make the lime syrup. Combine the ingredients in a small pan, bring to the boil, then simmer for 2–3 minutes until the sugar has dissolved and it has a syrupy texture. Set aside to cool until just warm. Once both sponges and syrup are slightly warm, brush the syrup over the sponges.

6 Shortly before you're ready to assemble the cake, remove your curd from the fridge and give it a whisk to loosen the texture slightly. Separately, whisk the double cream and icing sugar to soft peaks, then fold through the sour cream.

7 To assemble, place one of the sponges on a serving plate. Spread with a layer of cream, ensuring the cream is higher around the sides so that it can hold in the curd. Fill the trough with the curd, then repeat with the second sponge. Place the third sponge on top and spread this with a layer of cream. Garnish with toasted coconut and serve immediately.

Tip Topping cakes with a circle of greasepeoof paper can help them rise more evenly, which is particularly useful for cakes that you're planning to stack.

vanilla

rice porridge with rhubarb + vanilla **135**

milky bar basque cheesecake **136**

little vanilla bean pots with plums **138**

vanilla apricots with a hot sugar crust **140**

hot 'n' cold berries with white chocolate + cardamom **141**

simple citrus, olive oil + vanilla loaf **142**

white chocolate, miso + sesame cookies **144**

big molten chocolate soufflé **146**

green apple, vanilla + basil tart **148**

When I asked my friend Octavia, a chocolatier, how she felt about vanilla, her response was: 'Can we start with the fact that describing something plain/dull/boring as "vanilla" is the biggest miscarriage of justice *ever*?' I would have to agree. Vanilla is floral, woody, sweet, spicy, fruity, earthy – sometimes even smoky. Is it a sign of our supreme privilege that the intoxicating essence of a fruit that grows from an orchid has become pedestrian? At some point, somehow, vanilla became the layover flight to more exotic flavour destinations and what a shame that is: not only because vanilla is a remarkable flavour but because growing it is a troubling business, rife with risks for farmers. It may be the world's second-most-expensive spice (worth more than silver in 2018), yet those who grow it commercially get paid little. We shouldn't be taking it for granted.

Vanilla is native to Mexico, though very little is grown there now, such have been the devastating effects of deforestation. The Aztec civilisation used vanilla in many ways: for rituals, as incense to perfume temples during ceremonies, and in drinks such as atole (a warm cornmeal drink) and xocoatl ('bitter water', made of ground cocoa beans, chilli and corn). Eventually, vanilla pods were shipped to Europe (and beyond) by Spanish conquistadors in the sixteenth century, but two significant factors limited its cultivation in Europe. The first was climate: vanilla requires hot and wet conditions (21–32°C/70–90°F, 80% humidity), but also a degree of shelter and support from surrounding plants. The second was pollination: vanilla is a prim and fussy orchid, so while it possesses both male and female organs (which, in theory, could lead to self-pollination), there is a thin membrane between them which necessitates pollination by a third party. In Mexico, the little Melipona bee had been doing the job of pollination – but it did not exist elsewhere. Add to this that vanilla pods only open up for pollination for a single day and it's no wonder that, for decades after vanilla was transported beyond Mexico, reproduction was non-existent. That's where Edmond Albius enters the story.

On current-day Réunion, an island off the coast of Madagascar (previously Île de Bourbon, hence 'Bourbon vanilla'), a French botanist and slave-owner had a garden, some vanilla vines and some slaves, one of whom was a 12-year-old boy called Edmond. For years the mystery of how to get vanilla vines to produce fruit had flummoxed Europeans; however, Edmond showed promise as a botanist's assistant (unpaid) and figured out that by piercing the membrane between the vanilla plant's male and female organs, he could gently push them together ('the marriage'). This single discovery fuelled the wide availability of vanilla, an industry worth billions of dollars today: we owe much to a 12-year-old slave who eventually died in poverty.

From the point at which vanilla pods are picked – green, around 15–25cm (6–10in) long – there is still much work to do: the pods go through a lengthy process of curing, drying and conditioning, during which time vanillin develops, the chemical compound responsible for the flavour that we recognise. This process can take months. Harvesting vanilla is extremely labour and time intensive. Madagascar currently produces 80% of the world's vanilla and that's because, to put it bluntly, it's a country where the cost of labour is low enough (78% of Madagascans live on less than US$1.90 per day). Growing vanilla is risky business here, not just because cyclones and drought can devastate crops, but because international prices can swing significantly (a price crash in 2020 saw Madagascar rush to set a $350/kg minimum floor to stop its economy collapsing). And yet, even when the price plunges, it remains highly valuable, which makes vanilla heists common: farmers sometimes sleep by their crops with machetes to keep thieves at bay, although many have lost their lives trying to defend this heady spice. Vanilla is far from trivial – and anything but boring.

Practically speaking, it's useful to know when to splurge on vanilla. I don't keep multiple forms in my baking cupboard (because: space), so I mainly use vanilla bean paste since it's a best-of-both-worlds situation: fragrant and flecked with vanilla seeds, while having a stable shelf life. It's not cheap, though, so I am judicious in my use of it. Vanilla bean paste is largely wasted in cakes (other than very plain ones like the French Yoghurt Pot Loaf on page 160) because the flavour compounds evaporate, and vanilla can easily be dominated by other flavours. When it comes to cakes, vanilla pulls its weight far more in the buttercream, or in the whipped cream that you serve alongside, than it does in the sponge itself. Where the use of vanilla bean paste – or fresh pods – comes into its own is in milky, custardy desserts (crème brûlée, vanilla ice cream, canelé, etc.), fruit compotes and certain chocolate desserts (e.g. chocolate mousse). And while on the topic of chocolate, I must confess that white chocolate – which typically has some form of vanilla flavour added to it – makes an appearance as a vanilla sub in this chapter. Much like vanilla, white chocolate gets a bad rap for being 'basic', but when paired with the right flavours (think tart berries, cardamom, tangy cream cheese), it is truly knockout.

rice porridge with rhubarb + vanilla

This will make more rhubarb-vanilla compote than you need, but – trust me – you'll be glad of it and it'll keep in a sealed container or jar in the fridge for at least a week (so you could make it in advance, if you like).

If you don't have pudding rice, arborio could be substituted at a push, but bear in mind that it may take longer to cook.

balancing elements
rhubarb (sour)
salt

Every culture has some form of rice porridge or pudding: from Indian kheer to Greek rizogalo, from Sri Lankan pongal to Norwegian risgrøt. But here's the truth: this recipe is inspired by none of those. It's inspired, instead, by the memory of eating rice pudding out of a can with my friends after school – we loved the stuff. I wanted to find a way of eating rice pudding for breakfast (that is, everyday) and ended up with this recipe: vegan and low in sugar, but no less delicious for it!

Serves 2–3

150g (5oz/⅔ cup) pudding rice
700ml (1¼ pints/3 cups) rice milk
½ tsp vanilla bean paste
¼ tsp fine sea salt
100ml (3½fl oz/generous ⅓ cup) oat cream
1 tbsp maple syrup, or to taste

for the compote
450g (1lb) rhubarb, chopped into 2cm (¾in) pieces
120g (4½oz/½ cup plus 2 tbsp) caster (superfine) or granulated sugar
1 tsp vanilla bean paste

1 Place all the ingredients for the porridge, except the maple syrup, into a medium saucepan and set over a medium heat. Allow to simmer gently, stirring every so often, until the rice is cooked and the mixture has thickened, around 30 minutes. When you're happy with the consistency, sweeten the porridge to taste with the maple syrup. At this point, either keep it warm or transfer to the fridge to chill (my preference).

2 For the compote, add the ingredients to a small saucepan, cover with a lid and set over a medium-low heat until the rhubarb's natural juices are released, around 10 minutes. Remove the lid and gently simmer until thickened and slightly jammy, around 10–15 minutes.

3 To serve, divide the rice porridge between bowls, then top with a spoonful of the rhubarb-vanilla compote.

milky bar basque cheesecake

The best/closest flavour to Milky Bar comes from Meunier white cooking chocolate – I strongly recommend.

Philadelphia cream cheese is essential for cheesecakes as it is sufficiently stable.

An overnight rest in the fridge is essential for the best texture.

I like to use a 20cm (8in) tin in order to get a deep slice – fair warning, it will be pretty full but it won't spill over when baking; however, you could use a 23cm (9in) tin if you prefer

balancing elements
cream cheese (sour/tangy)
sour cream (sour/tangy)
burnt top (bitter)
salt

Serves 8–10

for the ganache
200g (7oz) white chocolate, finely chopped
360ml (12fl oz/1½ cups) double (heavy) cream

for the cheesecake
840g (1lb 14oz) full-fat cream cheese (3 x 280g/10oz family packs)
100g (3½oz/scant ½ cup) sour cream
140g (4¾oz/⅔ cup) caster (superfine) sugar
4 large eggs
40g (1½oz/3 heaped tbsp) cornflour (cornstarch)
1 tsp flaky sea salt
2 tsp vanilla bean paste
2 tsp fresh lemon juice

equipment
20cm (8in) springform cake tin

Also affectionately known as THE cheesecake.

1 Preheat the oven to 240°C fan/260°C/500°F/gas 10.

2 Press a large piece of greaseproof paper roughly into your springform tin (this doesn't have to be neat or elegant – just make sure that it reaches up and slightly over the sides).

3 For the ganache, add the chopped chocolate to a bowl. Gently heat the double cream in a saucepan until hot, then pour over the chopped chocolate and stir until fully melted. Set aside.

4 In a large bowl, briefly whisk together the cream cheese and sour cream until smooth, then add in the sugar and whisk until dissolved. (The aim is to combine everything, not whisk air into the mix – so avoid any sort of 'whipping cream' action.) Whisk in the eggs, one at a time, followed by the white chocolate ganache.

5 Sift the cornflour into a separate small bowl, then add the salt. Add 2–3 large spoonfuls of the cheesecake mix and whisk until there are no lumps. Add this thicker mixture back into the main cheesecake mix (use a spatula to ensure you don't leave any behind), then whisk together.

6 Lastly, add the vanilla and lemon juice, and use a spatula to ensure that everything has been fully combined.

7 Pour the mix into your prepared tin and bake until puffed up, blackened on top and reasonably jiggly in the middle – the reality is that the baking time will vary a lot depending on the fierceness of your oven, so this is one to trust your instincts on. Start checking from the 30-minute mark, and rest assured that a good wobble in the middle is okay as the white chocolate ganache helps it to firm up considerably in the fridge. I find the sweet spot is around the 35-minute mark.

8 Allow to cool to room temperature, then store in the fridge overnight. I love eating a Basque cold, but you can also bring it to room temperature (it will have a softer set/won't slice as nicely if you do this).

Tip Every cheesecake benefits from an overnight stint in the fridge, tempting though it is to eat it immediately – it's this step that ensures a luscious, creamy texture. See also: Piña Colada Cheeseake (page 127).

little vanilla bean pots with plums

For extra richness, you could replace some of the milk with cream, but I like the restraint of this version.

Avoid using rich-yolk eggs for this, as they can give the custard a pink-ish hue.

The custard requires several hours in the fridge (overnight, ideally). The plums can be made in advance and gently reheated.

Star anise is a match made in heaven with plums, but could be left out if preferred.

balancing elements
plums (sour)
star anise (herbal/aniseed)

Custard is so often thought of as a filling (for tarts, eclairs, profiteroles, etc.) or the accompaniment to the main dessert, but sometimes custard can – and should – simply be the dessert. I guess that's what the French inherently understood when they created little pots de crèmes. These chilled ramekins of silky, vanilla-flecked custard are completely delicious as they are, but adorned with some warm baked plums? Truly, you could not ask for more.

Makes 8

700ml (1¼ pints/3 cups) whole milk
80g (3oz/generous ⅓ cup) caster (superfine) sugar
1 vanilla pod (or 1 tbsp vanilla bean paste)
1 egg
5 egg yolks
¼ tsp fine sea salt

for the maple plums
25g (1oz) butter
3 tbsp maple syrup
1 star anise
8 plums, halved and pitted

equipment
8 x 150ml (5fl oz/⅔ cup) ceramic or glass ramekins (or similar)
a large baking dish

1 Preheat the oven to 150°C fan/170°C/340°F/gas 3. Boil the kettle.

2 Add the milk to a medium saucepan along with half of the sugar (eyeball this!) and the vanilla. Heat over a medium heat until steaming.

3 Meanwhile, whisk together the egg and yolks with the remaining sugar and the salt in a large bowl. Whisk in a quarter of the steaming milk mixture, followed by the rest. Pour the custard mixture into the ramekins, then tap them gently on the counter to get rid of excess air bubbles. Sit them into the bigger baking dish, place on the middle shelf of the oven and gently pour the boiled water around them until it reaches halfway up the sides. Bake until the custard just wobbles slightly in the middle, around 25 minutes (baking times may vary depending on the type/material/thickness of the ramekins that you use). Remove from the oven and set aside to cool, then transfer to the fridge for at least a couple of hours, ideally overnight.

4 For the plums, preheat the oven to 170°C fan/190°C/375°F/gas 5. Add the butter, maple syrup and star anise to a lipped baking tray (sufficient to hold the plum halves in a single layer) and place in the oven for 2–3 minutes to allow the butter to melt. Remove from the oven, swirl together the butter and maple syrup, then add the plums, cut-sides down. Turn all the plum halves over, then return the tray to the oven and roast for 20 minutes until the plums have softened and started to release their juices. Allow to cool for 5 minutes before serving one or two halves on top of each custard.

Tip Any baked custard (e.g. crème brûlée, cheesecake) is much improved by an overnight stint in the fridge – it helps the proteins in the egg to settle, which contributes to a silky-smooth texture. See also: Black Sugar Crème Caramel (page 39).

vanilla apricots with a hot sugar crust

To make this coeliac-friendly, swap the flour for gluten-free flour.

I like the tartness of the unsweetened apricots against the sweet hot sugar crust, but if you have a sweet tooth add a tablespoon or two of sugar to the fruit.

This is a super-versatile recipe that works brilliantly with other fruit – particularly tart stone fruit such as plums, but also apples, pears and rhubarb.

balancing element
apricots (sour)

Sometimes a recipe can read like an act of self-sabotage (`You're telling me that we're making meringues out of chickpea water?'; `Are you seriously asking me to put mayonnaise in my chocolate cake?'; etc.). And arguably, the method for this hot sugar crust reads the same way: you might reasonably feel that chucking boiling water over cake batter would be a recipe for disaster. But the reality is different. It's a technique that creates an amazing crackly-textured top that contrasts with the soft apricots and cake underneath. And while vanilla, like a pair of classic jeans, goes with almost everything sweet, it particularly shines against fruits with decent acidity – in this case beautiful apricots.

Serves 4

600g (1lb 5oz) apricots, pitted
   and halved
seeds from 1 vanilla pod
   (or 1½ tsp vanilla bean paste)
zest and juice of ½ lemon
¼ tsp fine sea salt

for the hot sugar crust
55g (2¼oz) butter
90g (3¼oz/scant ½ cup)
   granulated sugar,
   plus 3 tbsp for the top
100g (3½oz/generous ¾ cup)
   plain (all-purpose) flour
1 tsp baking powder
¼ tsp fine sea salt
90ml (3fl oz/⅓ cup plus 2 tsp) milk
60ml (2½fl oz/¼ cup) freshly
   boiled water

equipment
baking dish to snugly fit the apricots
   in a double layer
electric hand whisk

1   Preheat the oven to 170°C fan/190°C/375°F/gas 5.

2   Chop the apricot halves into 4 pieces, then add to the baking dish along with the vanilla, lemon zest and juice, and salt. Toss it all together.

3   Cream the butter with the 90g (3¼oz/scant ½ cup) of sugar until combined and creamy but still sandy in texture (we're *not* looking to dissolve the sugar, like you would when making a cake), around 1 minute. Add the dry ingredients and mix until incorporated (the mix will go crumbly). Add half of the milk and combine, then add the rest and beat the mixture until light and fluffy, around 2 minutes.

4   Add the batter to the apricots in the dish in large spoonfuls, then use an offset spatula (or back of a spoon) to spread and level it out – you want most of the fruit to be covered with around 1cm (½in) of batter, no more. Sprinkle the additional 3 tbsp of sugar over the top of the batter, then drizzle the hot water evenly over the top.

5   Bake until the top is golden and crackled, around 1 hour 10 minutes – but do start checking from the 50-minute mark. You should expect the edges to turn a darker, more caramelised colour but the centre to remain a burnished gold. Remove from the oven and allow to cool for 10 minutes before serving.

hot 'n' cold berries with white chocolate + cardamom

Avoid including strawberries in the mix of frozen berries – they are too large and watery for this.

balancing elements
raspberries (tart)
blackcurrants (tart/sour)
cardamom (subtly bitter/herbal)
bay leaf (herbal/aniseed)

The Scandinavian frozen berries with white chocolate sauce from The Ivy is possibly the simplest and most perfect of desserts: cold, tart, toothsome frozen berries are topped with a hot, rich, smooth white chocolate sauce and when they meet . . . fireworks. It's incredibly simple to pull off (read: perfect for a dinner party) and knockout to eat. I have messed with it very little other than to introduce musky cardamom and fragrant bay to the equation, flavours that were made for the milky, vanilla notes of white chocolate.

Serves 4–6

10 cardamom pods
300ml (10fl oz/1⅓ cups) double (heavy) cream
3 bay leaves
300g (10½oz) white chocolate, finely chopped
750g (1lb 10oz) mixed, small frozen berries (blackcurrants, raspberries, etc.)

1 Bash the cardamom pods a little to break them open, then add to a medium saucepan along with the double cream. Tear the bay leaves in half (to release their flavour) and add to the cream. Heat until steaming, then set aside to steep for 30 minutes.

2 Strain out the bay leaves and cardamom, then return the cream to the pan and heat to just shy of boiling. Take off the heat and add the chopped white chocolate (which should be fully submerged). Leave for a minute before whisking until the white chocolate is melted. Place back over a very low heat until you are ready to serve.

3 To serve, remove the frozen berries from the freezer and arrange on a large platter in a single layer (or you could plate up individually). Leave for 3 minutes or so, to take the edge of the frost off. Transfer the hot white chocolate sauce to a jug. Take the platter of berries to the table, then pour over the hot sauce and eat immediately.

simple citrus, olive oil + vanilla loaf

I love this best with blood oranges, but it could also be made with standard oranges, clementines, grapefruits or lemons (or a mix).

balancing elements
Greek yoghurt (sour/tangy)
olive oil (bitter)
blood oranges (tart)
lemon juice (sour)

Makes 8–10 slices

2 blood oranges, plus the juice
  of ½ blood orange
  (about 20–30ml/¾–1fl oz/
  1½–2 tablespoons)
2 eggs
110ml (3½fl oz/scant ½ cup)
  olive oil
80g (3oz/⅓ cup) Greek yoghurt,
  plus extra to serve
juice of ½ lemon
1 tsp vanilla bean paste
140g (4¾oz/⅔ cup) caster
  (superfine) or granulated sugar
100g (3½oz/generous ¾ cup)
  plain (all-purpose) flour
¾ tsp baking powder
¼ tsp bicarbonate of soda
  (baking soda)
¼ tsp fine sea salt

for the syrup
juice of 2 blood oranges
  (about 80ml/2½fl oz/⅓ cup)
80g (3oz/generous ⅓ cup) caster
  (superfine) or granulated sugar
½ tsp vanilla bean paste

equipment
1 x 900g (2lb) loaf tin

A joyous one-bowl affair that will bring colour and zing to winter days.

1 Preheat the oven to 160°C fan/180°C/350°F/gas 4 and line the loaf tin.

2 Zest the two oranges and set the zest aside, then top and tail them, removing the skin and pith by running a knife down the sides. Slice the oranges crossways into 5mm (¼in) rounds, picking out and discarding the pips. Arrange in the bottom of the loaf tin in a single layer (you may not need all the slices, depending on the size of your oranges).

3 In a jug, whisk together the eggs, olive oil, yoghurt, orange zest and juice, lemon juice and vanilla.

4 Separately, whisk together the sugar, flour, baking powder, bicarbonate of soda and salt in a medium bowl. Pour the wet ingredients into the dry ingredients and mix until combined.

5 Pour the batter into the prepared loaf tin and bake until a skewer comes out clean, around 45 minutes. Allow to cool for 5–10 minutes, then turn out onto a wire cooling rack.

6 To make the syrup, combine the orange juice, sugar and vanilla in a pan and bring to the boil. Simmer for 2–3 minutes until slightly thickened, then remove from the heat and set aside to cool for 5 minutes.

7 To serve, turn the loaf upside down (so that the oranges are visible) and brush the syrup over the top. Serve slices with a dollop of Greek yoghurt.

Tip Loaf tin liners are available in most major supermarkets and will make your baking life infinitely easier! See also: French Yoghurt Pot Loaf on page 160.

white chocolate, miso + sesame cookies

This dough requires a rest in the fridge before baking. Alternatively, it can be made ahead, frozen and then baked directly from the freezer. (Be very careful when slicing through a frozen log of cookie dough!)

These will keep for up to 5 days stored in an airtight container.

For extra toasty/funky flavour, replace the white chocolate with a caramelised version (e.g. Valrhona Dulcey Blond).

balancing elements
salted butter (salty)
white miso (sweet/salty/umami)
white sesame seeds (subtly bitter)
black sesame seeds (subtle umami)
dark muscovado (subtle acidity)

When you think of cookies, you don't usually think of words like 'funky' and 'complex', but if there were ever a cookie that matched those descriptors then this is it. My friend Octavia and I served a version of these at our chocolate-themed pop up (Cocoa POP!) and, frankly, they're addictive. Adapted from a recipe by Nicola Lamb, Octavia's addition of white miso adds a funkiness that plays brilliantly against the chocolate, while my addition of sesame seeds contributes visual appeal as well as a savoury backnote.

Makes 11–12 cookies

120g (4½oz) salted butter
40g (1½oz) white miso
  (I like MisoTasty)
110g (4oz/generous ½ cup)
  caster (superfine) sugar
40g (1½oz/2 heaped tbsp)
  dark muscovado
  (or soft dark brown) sugar
½ tsp bicarbonate of soda
  (baking soda)
2 large egg yolks
170g (6oz/generous 1¼ cups)
  plain (all-purpose) flour
140g (4¾oz) white chocolate,
  roughly chopped
20g (¾oz) sesame seeds (a mix
  of black and white is nice)

equipment
electric hand whisk
silicone baking mats
  (or greaseproof paper)
large round cookie cutter, for
  'scooting' (helpful, not essential)

1   Briefly cream together the butter, miso, both sugars and the bicarb using an electric whisk (you want it to lighten slightly, but we're not looking to cream this properly, like you would for a cake). Next, briefly whisk in the egg yolks, followed by the flour. Fold through the white chocolate.

2   Transfer the dough to a sheet of cling film (plastic wrap) and shape it into a log around 6cm (2¼in) wide. Seal the log in the cling film and roll it under your hands to help smooth out the shape. Chill in the fridge for at least 3 hours, or overnight.

3   When ready to bake, preheat the oven to 170°C fan/190°C/375°F/gas 5. Line a couple of baking trays (if you only have one baking tray, bake the cookies in batches).

4   Slice the dough log into 1.5cm (¾in) rounds (these should weigh around 60g/2¼oz each) and place on the baking trays, leaving a decent amount of space around each. Sprinkle each cookie with sesame seeds and then bake until golden around the edges, around 12–13 minutes. For perfectly round biscuits, as soon as they are out of the oven take the cookie cutter, place it around each biscuit in turn, gently moving it in a circular motion to nudge them into a rounded shape (this is called 'scooting'). Transfer to a wire rack to cool.

Tip Any biscuit or cookie dough, as well as pastry, hugely benefits from an overnight rest in the fridge. This ensures that the flour is properly hydrated and the gluten has had a chance to relax. What this means for you is dough that is easier to work with and gives a better result when baked (less spread, more height). See also: Terrazzo Cookies (page 40).

big molten chocolate soufflé

I like to use Guittard semi-sweet chocolate chips for this, because they have a higher cocoa percentage than standard milk chocolate. But if milk chocolate is what you have/can find, then simply up the dark chocolate to 220g/7oz and reduce the milk chocolate quantity to 50g/2oz.

balancing elements
dark chocolate (bitter)
cocoa powder (bitter)
salt

Soufflés are often associated with formal dining rooms and individual plates of food. But one BIG chocolate soufflé plonked in the middle of the table at the end of a meal? That's impressive yet casual, exciting yet familial – said another way: it's a bloody great way to end a dinner party. And though the chocolate is the star here, vanilla makes a subtle but fragrant backnote to the cocoa, enhancing its subtly exotic flavours.

Serves 6

for the soufflé
50g (2oz) butter, melted
40g (1½oz/3 tbsp) caster (superfine) sugar, plus extra to coat the dish
10 egg whites

for the pastry cream
525ml (18fl oz/2¼ cups) whole milk
140g (4¾oz/⅔ cup) caster (superfine) sugar
6 egg yolks
30g (1oz/2 heaped tbsp) cornflour (cornstarch)
30g (1oz/2 heaped tbsp) cocoa powder
½ tsp fine sea salt
1 tbsp vanilla bean paste
190g (6¾oz) dark chocolate (at least 70% cocoa solids), finely chopped
80g (3¼oz) milk (semi-sweet) chocolate (around 46% cocoa solids), finely chopped

for the cream
400ml (14fl oz/1¾ cups) double (heavy) cream
3 tbsp icing (confectioners') sugar, sifted, plus extra for dusting
1 tbsp vanilla bean paste

equipment
large ramekin or serving dish – about 1.5 litres (2½ pints) capacity
electric hand whisk

1 Prepare the soufflé dish by brushing the melted butter up the sides, then place it in the fridge to set for 5–10 minutes. Brush on another layer of melted butter, then coat with caster sugar, tapping out any excess. Place in the fridge to set.

2 Next, make the pastry cream. Heat the milk and half of the sugar in a pan until the sugar has dissolved and the milk is steaming.

3 In a separate bowl, whisk together the egg yolks with the remaining sugar to ribbon stage, then whisk in the cornflour, cocoa powder and salt. Whisk a third of the milk mixture into the bowl of egg yolks, then pour the egg yolk mixture into the remaining milk in the pan. Add the vanilla bean paste and whisk continuously until the mixture has thickened. Remove the custard from the heat and add the finely chopped chocolate, whisking until fully melted. Transfer the pastry cream to a medium mixing bowl and cover the surface with a layer of cling film (plastic wrap), then place in the fridge to chill for 20 minutes.

4 When ready to bake, preheat the oven to 190°C fan/210°C/400°F/gas 7, adding a flat baking tray in there to heat up at the same time.

5 In a large stainless-steel bowl, beat the egg whites with an electric hand whisk until frothy. Continuing to whisk, add the 40g (1½oz/3 tablespoons) of caster sugar a spoonful at a time until the mixture reaches soft peaks.

6 Whisk a third of the egg whites into the pastry cream to loosen, then gently fold in another third, taking care not to knock out the air. Fold in the last third, then transfer the mix to the prepared dish (it should reach the top, but if you have any extra, simply bake it off in small ramekins). Transfer the dish to the hot baking tray and bake until well risen and set around the edges, around 45–50 minutes. Try not to open the door while the soufflé is cooking but do keep an eye on it through the glass, turning the oven down if you see (or smell) the top getting too brown.

7 While the soufflé is baking, whip the cream with the icing sugar and vanilla until it holds. Once the soufflé is cooked, dust it with icing sugar and transfer it directly to the dinner table, adding a large dollop of the vanilla cream to the top of the soufflé, and serving the rest alongside.

green apple, vanilla + basil tart

The vanilla-basil sugar will keep in a cool, dark place for several weeks, so you can make it in advance. This'll make more than you need for the tart.

If you can, opt for an all-butter puff pastry – I like the Dorset brand. Puff pastry brands vary slightly in size, so you may find you need more or fewer apples.

Best served warm with a pour of cold single (light) or double (heavy) cream.

balancing elements
green apple (sour/tart)
basil (herbal)

I first came across the combination of vanilla and basil in an ice-cream parlour in Lisbon and the memory has never left me. It's a surprisingly natural combination that adds a beautiful note of interest to this rustic apple frangipane tart. The idea and method for this flavoured herb sugar came from the wonderful and brilliant Mark Diacono.

Serves 6–8

for the vanilla-basil sugar
40g (1½oz) basil leaves
50g (2oz/¼ cup) caster (superfine) sugar
seeds from 1 vanilla pod

for the frangipane
50g (2oz) butter, softened
50g (2oz/¼ cup) caster (superfine) sugar
small pinch of baking powder
1 egg
40g (1½oz/generous ⅓ cup) ground almonds
1 tbsp cornflour (cornstarch)
1 tbsp amaretto (or ¼ tsp almond extract), if liked

for the tart
1 x sheet of store-bought puff pastry
3 Granny Smith apples, cored
25g (1oz) salted butter, melted
1 egg, beaten, for brushing

1   Preheat the oven to 110°C fan/130°C/275°F/gas 1.

2   Roughly tear the basil, then crush it in a mortar and pestle or spice blender until it becomes a paste. Spread over a piece of greaseproof paper on a baking tray and place in the oven for 30 minutes, forking through it halfway through to ensure it all dries out evenly. Allow to cool, then blitz in a small blender along with the sugar and vanilla to create a fine, bright green dust.

3   To make the frangipane, cream the butter, sugar and baking powder together until light and fluffy, 1–2 minutes (it might take a while to come together). Next, beat in the egg. Add the ground almonds and cornflour, then fold this into the batter just until combined. Stir in the amaretto (or almond extract), if using.

4   When you're ready to start putting together the tart, preheat the oven to 180°C fan/200°C/400°F/gas 6.

5   Roll out the sheet of puff pastry onto a greaseproof-lined baking tray and cut it in half lengthways, so that you have two long strips of pastry. Lightly score a 1cm (½in) border around the edge of each pastry rectangle, then spread the frangipane within the borders using an offset spatula (or back of a spoon). Place in the fridge to chill while you prep the apples.

6   Halve the apples, then finely slice them crossways, around 2mm (⅛in) thick (if you have a mandoline, it makes this job particularly quick).

7   Arrange the apple slices along the length of each pastry base, allowing them to overlap. Brush with melted butter, then sprinkle over 1 tablespoon of the vanilla-basil sugar. Brush the borders with egg wash. Bake until the pastry is golden and the apples are soft, around 30 minutes. Allow to cool for 10 minutes before slicing and serving.

milk +
honey

On the east coast of Spain there is a Mesolithic cave painting that's over 8,000 years old. Etched into the walls is an illustration of human beings climbing a sheer cliff in order to get to a hive, with bees swarming around ready to defend their precious stores – such were the lengths that humans would go to get hold of the original sweetener, honey. This liquid gold – the stored food of bees – is the most concentrated natural source of sweetness that exists, and flavour-wise it is magic: ambrosial, aromatic, often floral, sometimes woody, it is a liquid sweetener that echoes the local terroir of the bees. Honey contains bee enzymes, polyphenols, over 30 different flavonoids and all nine essential amino acids – and this is what makes it remarkable, not only in flavour but also in function.

Before refined white sugar was ubiquitous and readily available, fruit and honey were our limited sources of sweetness, which explains why honey has come to carry tremendous religious and anthropological significance over the years. There is no major civilisation or religion that has not prized honey in some shape or form. The Ancient Egyptians believed honey came from the god Ra ('his tears fell to the ground and were turned into bees', according to an Egyptian papyrus) and they used it in medical prescriptions and to embalm corpses. The Ancient Greeks offered honey in ceremonies to the dead and the gods. In the Christian New Testament, John the Baptist lived for a long period in the wilderness on a diet of locusts and wild honey. In the Qur'an there is a chapter called 'al Nahl' – 'the honeybee' – and the Prophet Muhammad recommended honey for healing. In Hinduism, honey is one of the five foods used for worship, while in Judaism it is a symbol of the New Year, Rosh Hashana. Moreover, the great tradition of beekeeping in Europe in the Middle Ages was driven by a need, not just for honey but for beeswax, to light the great churches and cathedrals. Honey has meant (and still means) a lot to many.

Bees are one of the oldest forms of animal life, preceding humans on Earth by 10–20 million years, but once it became clear to humans – around 5,000 years ago – that honey was a product of bees, the practice of beekeeping started up. The Ancient Egyptians were the first to carry out beekeeping on a large, commercial scale, producing thousands of tonnes of honey a year. Hives would be placed on barges travelling up and down the Nile to track the big flowering events. The Egyptians domesticated what we know as the Western honeybee and, initially, it was able to produce enough honey for the bees and for us (today it's a different story). For thousands of years, then, honey was the main deal – and this only changed when sugar came onto the scene (see page 11).

Today, it's hard to imagine a world where honey would be viewed as anything other than a supplementary sweetener, although its health credentials ought to make us take note. Honey is a remarkable natural substance: antibacterial, anti-inflammatory and scientifically proven to improve allergies (by exposing you to local pollen in tiny amounts). Studies have even shown that it can reduce the occurrence of dementia (a study of 4,000 subjects, 65 and over, who ate 1 tablespooon of honey a day, saw a 400% greater incidence of dementia in the placebo group). It's also a powerful preservative, on account of its slight acidity, high sugar and low water content. Over the millennia, honey has been put to use in myriad ways: in food and drink (e.g. to glaze meats, to make mead), as medicine and in religious ceremonies. It has even been used as a war tool: the honey made of flowers from certain plants can be toxic to humans, and there is evidence that armies planted honey to place the opposition into a stupor – one man's liquid gold, another man's poison. Today, its power lies in its ability to contribute additional layers of flavour to desserts and bakes – honey is far from one-note.

Naturally, the biblical reference to 'a land flowing with milk and honey' inspired this chapter, and so we don't just cover honey-sweetened treats in these pages but also desserts and bakes that feature milk in its many forms – from infused (Cereal Milk Panna Cotta, page 156), to caramelised (No-Churn Dulce de Leche Ice Cream, page 167), to soured (Raspberries + Sour Cream, page 154). Cream as the basis of custards and panna cottas, or simple fruit-based desserts, is probably familiar territory, but less familiar might be the wonderful effects of milk or cream *in* cakes, or the alchemy that occurs when you deliberately burn the stuff. Milk, it turns out, is not just the primary accompaniment to cookies – it possesses two qualities that can really enhance baking and desserts: fat and natural sugars. Both of these equate to better flavour and texture. So the next time you're making a Victoria sponge, don't skip the step of loosening the batter with milk (or even better, swap the milk for double/heavy cream): the sponge will be subtly but undoubtedly enhanced, made more plush and more delicious. Milk is capable of producing myriad (baking) miracles in the kitchen.

raspberries + sour cream

This dish is easily scaled up or down according to how many people you're serving. It can also be made in one larger dish instead of individual ramekins.

balancing elements
raspberries (tart)
sour cream (sour/tangy)
caramelised sugar (subtly bitter)

I'll be honest: this a barely a recipe. It's just one of those simple preparations that is so much greater than the sum of its parts that I feel compelled to share it with you. The fruity sourness of raspberries against the rich, lactic tang of sour cream, all balanced by a scant spoonful of caramel-like muscovado sugar, makes for a divine and light end to any meal. All credit for this concept to Jeremiah Tower's eighties cookbook New American Classics.

Serves 4–6

200g (7oz) fresh raspberries
120g (4½oz/½ cup)
   sour cream (full-fat)
4 tbsp light muscovado
   (or soft light brown) sugar

equipment
4–6 ramekins, depending on size
   (I use 10cm/4in ramekins, which
   gives me 4 servings)

1 Preheat your grill to its highest setting.

2 Add the raspberries to your ramekins roughly in a single layer, then top each with 2 tablespoons of sour cream, using a small offset spatula (or the back of a spoon) to gently spread the cream until it mostly covers the raspberries. Evenly scatter a tablespoon of sugar over each ramekin, then pop the dishes under the grill until the sugar just starts to caramelise. Serve immediately.

cereal milk panna cotta

Panna cottas require several hours in the fridge to set, so I typically make them the day before I'm serving them.

The caramelised cornflakes can be made up to 3 days ahead and stored in an airtight container.

The grade of gelatine that you use is really important – do make sure it's platinum.

coffee (bitter)
light muscovado (subtle acidity)

You can't go too far wrong with a panna cotta – even an average one is a nice thing – and yet it's certainly within everyone's reach to make a divine one. The trick is using just enough gelatine so that they set without taking on a jelly-like texture, as well as balancing out the double (heavy) cream with some milk and water to preserve some lightness.

Inspired by a dessert I had on MasterChef when returning to judge the 2023 class, cereal milk as a concept was created by Christina Tosi (of Milk Bar fame), inspired by the sweetened milk that you get at the end of a bowl of cereal. Its genius lies in the fact that it tastes of childhood while also having a slightly malty, not-too-sweet, grown-up flavour.

Serves 6

40g (1½oz) cornflakes
60g (2oz/⅓ cup) light muscovado (or soft light brown) sugar
450ml (15fl oz/1¾ cups) whole milk
2 leaves of platinum-grade fine leaf gelatine (I use Dr Oetker)
75ml (2¾fl oz/⅓ cup) double (heavy) cream

for the caramelised cornflakes
20g (¾oz) butter
1½ tsp maple syrup
¼ tsp flaky sea salt
½ tsp ground coffee
25g (¾oz) cornflakes

equipment
6 x 220ml (7½fl oz) dariole moulds (or similar ramekins/glasses)

1 Preheat the oven to 150°C fan/170°C/340°F/gas 3. Spread the 40g (1½oz) of cornflakes on a lined baking tray and bake until lightly toasted, around 20 minutes. Transfer to a small saucepan along with 1 tbsp/15g of the brown sugar and allow to cool before pouring over the milk and stirring everything together. Set this aside to steep for 30 minutes.

2 Reuse the lined baking tray for the caramelised cornflakes. Melt the butter, maple syrup, salt and coffee together in a small pan, then pour over the 25g (¾oz) of cornflakes and stir until well coated. Spread the cornflakes out on the baking tray and bake until golden, around 10 minutes. Cool, then store in an airtight container until needed.

3 Strain the cornflake-milk mixture into a jug to separate the cornflakes (don't attempt to squeeze additional milk out of the cornflakes, as you want to avoid collecting any starchy liquid). Rinse out the pan, then pour the infused milk mixture back into it. Rinse out your dariole moulds with water and tap out any excess (leaving them wet). Separately, cover your gelatine with cold water and leave to soak for a few minutes (this is called 'blooming').

4 Add the cream and the remaining brown sugar to the cornflake-infused milk and set over a medium heat until the mixture is steaming and the sugar has dissolved (you want it hot enough to activate the gelatine but not boiling, as this will affect the flavour and may also result in a skin). Remove your gelatine sheets from the water (they should now be soft) and whisk into the cream mixture – they should dissolve immediately.

5 Pour the mixture into your dariole moulds and place on a tray in the fridge to set – at least 3–4 hours, or overnight.

6 To serve, boil the kettle and leave it to cool for 5 minutes. Pour the hot water into a shallow dish. Dip each dariole mould into the hot water for 2–3 seconds, then invert onto a serving plate. Gently shake to help the panna cotta release – you should feel this happen, but if it doesn't just dip the mould back into the hot water for another second or two and try again. Sprinkle over the caramelised cornflakes and serve immediately.

berber 'nutella' (moroccan amlou)

Try to buy the freshest almonds you can find – I find Lidl to have some of the best nuts out of all the major supermarkets!

balancing elements
cardamom (subtly bitter)
salt

While peanut butter is far superior when crunchy, almonds – when turned into nut butter – are destined for silky smooth submission. Add argan oil and you turn average almond butter into a kind of liquid gold, which is clearly where Moroccans were going with this particular spread/ dip. Sweetened with honey and spiced with a little ground cardamom (my addition), this is a chill upgrade for your pantry that will seriously up your morning toast game.

Makes around 1–1½ jars

200g (7oz) skin-on almonds
¼ tsp flaky sea salt, plus
   extra to taste
100ml (3½fl oz/generous ⅓ cup)
   culinary argan oil
3–5 tbsp runny honey, to taste
¼–½ tsp ground cardamom,
   to taste

equipment
powerful blender
   (or food processor)
2 x sterilised jars

1   Preheat the oven to 140°C fan/160°C/325°F/gas 3.

2   Spread the almonds out on a large baking tray and toast in the oven for 40 minutes.

3   Add the toasted almonds and salt to a blender and process until it forms a smooth, almost pourable nut butter – this could take between 5 and 10 minutes, and you may want to scrape down the sides from time to time.

4   Once you have the almond butter, keep the blender running and slowly drizzle in the argan oil (like you would with a mayonnaise) until you have a gleaming, looser version of the nut butter.

5   Gently warm the honey in a pan until it loosens in texture, then add 3 tablespoons to the amlou along with ¼ teaspoon of the ground cardamom, blend and taste. Add more honey, a tablespoon at a time, to taste. You can also add more cardamom and salt if you like. Transfer to your sterilised jars and allow to cool before sealing with lids. Store in a cool, dark place.

little
lemon
+ honey
cakes

You can pipe this mix into silicone moulds and freeze prior to baking. Simply bake from frozen, for a little longer than stated below.

These are best eaten the day that they are made.

The edges of these kinds of cakes go darker and chewier, but if you want something more cupcake-like (lighter texture and colour), bake these in cupcake liners instead of directly in the tin.

balancing elements
lemon zest (bitter)
lemon juice (sour)
brown butter (subtle umami)

I have no idea why the popularity of financiers and friands – little French cakes made with ground almonds and egg whites – seems to be restricted to France, because they tick all the boxes: quick, easy, tasty (brown butter will do that) and a great use of excess egg whites.

Makes 6 small cakes

75g (3oz) butter, plus extra
    for greasing (if using a
    cupcake tin)
40g (1½oz/¼ cup plus 2 tbsp)
    plain (all-purpose) flour, plus extra
    for dusting
50g (2oz/2 tbsp) runny honey
    (a strong-flavoured one is nice)
30g (1oz/2½ tbsp)
    granulated sugar
50g (2oz/½ cup) ground almonds
¼ tsp baking powder
pinch of fine salt
zest of 1 lemon
2 egg whites

for the candied lemon peel
1 lemon
60ml (2¼fl oz/¼ cup) water
60g (2¼oz/¼ cup plus 1 tbsp) caster
    (superfine) sugar
1 tbsp granulated sugar

for the lemon glaze
juice of ½ lemon
1½ tsp runny honey
70g (3oz/¾ cup) icing
    (confectioners') sugar
1 tsp cornflour (cornstarch)

equipment
silicone financier or friand
    moulds, or a 12-hole,
    non-stick cupcake tin
piping bag (helpful, not essential)

1   Preheat the oven to 200°C fan/220°C/425°F/gas 7. If using a cupcake tin, grease the holes of your muffin tin with butter, dust with flour, then turn the tray upside down and tap any excess out. Place in the fridge to chill.

2   In a small metal saucepan (so that you can see it change colour), melt the butter over a low heat. Turn the heat up to medium and allow the butter to simmer gently until it turns golden and smells nutty, up to 10 minutes. Keep a constant eye on it to take it to a deeply toasted colour, removing it from the heat as soon as it's reached this level. Strain through a very fine sieve or piece of muslin to remove the milk solids, then stir through the honey until melted. Set aside.

3   Whisk together the flour, sugar, ground almonds, baking powder, salt and lemon zest in a medium bowl. Separately, whisk together the egg whites to soft peaks. Add the egg whites to the flour mixture and whisk until there are no dry bits. Whisk in the melted butter until combined. Fill a piping bag (if using) with the batter and divide equally among the holes in your silicone mould/cupcake tin (or simply spoon/pour it in).

4   Bake the cakes for 8 minutes, then turn the temperature down to 170°C fan/190°C/375°F/gas 5, turn the tray around, and bake until they are golden, the centres have peaked slightly and they spring back when gently prodded, a further 5–7 minutes. Allow to cool for a couple of minutes before turning out onto a wire rack to cool fully.

5   Meanwhile, make the candied lemon peel. Use a vegetable peeler to create wide strips of zest. Remove any large bits of white pith with a paring knife, then slice the zest into very thin strips. Line a baking tray with greaseproof paper. Add the water and caster sugar to a saucepan and bring to the boil. Add the strips of zest and simmer for 10 minutes or so until translucent. Remove from the syrup and arrange on the lined tray, ensuring all the strips of zest are separate. Leave to dry for an hour or so before tossing in the granulated sugar.

6   For the glaze, whisk together 2 teaspoons of the lemon juice and the honey in a small bowl, then sift in a third of the icing sugar. Whisk until completely smooth, then repeat with the rest of the icing sugar and cornflour. If the glaze is too thick, add more lemon juice, ½ teaspoon at a time. Once the cakes are cooled, spoon the icing over them, allowing it to run down the sides a little. Top each cake with some candied lemon peel, then set aside to allow the icing to set, around 30 minutes.

french
yoghurt
pot loaf

This is perfect for making with little ones (as my mum did with me and my brother) since it is easy and forgiving.

The vanilla is essential – don't skip it!

balancing elements
natural yoghurt (sour/tangy)
lemon zest (bitter)

No scales? No problem. This is the cake to make if you're baking with kids, or you're a student with limited equipment, or you've just moved into your first place and haven't equipped your kitchen yet. In fact, it's also perfect if you're just feeling lazy. You simply take a small pot of yoghurt, empty out the yoghurt into a bowl to start the cake batter and then use the empty pot to measure out the rest of the ingredients. It's the first cake I ever learnt to make and it's a deliciously comforting, easy bake. The yoghurt doesn't materially change the flavour but it gives more depth and a satisfying, plush texture.

Makes 1 loaf cake

1 x 150ml (5fl oz) pot of natural yoghurt
2 yoghurt pots of caster (superfine) or granulated sugar
1 yoghurt pot of sunflower or vegetable oil
3 eggs
2 tsp high-quality vanilla extract
2 tsp baking powder
½ tsp fine sea salt
3 yoghurt pots of plain (all-purpose) flour

equipment
900g (2lb) loaf tin

1 Preheat the oven to 180°C fan/200°C/400°F/gas 6 and line your loaf tin (see tip).

2 In a medium bowl, whisk together the yoghurt, sugar, oil, eggs, vanilla, baking powder and salt. Next, briefly whisk in the flour until most of the lumps have been removed from the batter.

3 Pour the batter into the prepared tin and bake for 30 minutes, before turning the oven down to 170°C fan/190°C/375°F/gas 5. Bake until a skewer inserted in the centre of the cake comes out clean, around 20 minutes more. Leave to cool for around 10 minutes before serving.

Tip Loaf tin liners are available in most major supermarkets and will make your baking life infinitely easier! See also: Simple Citrus, Olive Oil + Vanilla Loaf (page 142) and Vegan Coconut + Lime Loaf (page 125).

blackcurrant, bay + clotted cream cake

Blackcurrants aren't the easiest to get hold of but it's worth it for this. When in season (July–August in the UK), freeze them so that you have access year-round. Alternatively, buy bags of frozen blackcurrants online or use tinned, drained of their juice. If using tinned, drain them, reduce the sugar in the compote to 1 tablespoon and leave out the water.

balancing elements
blackcurrants (sour)
bay leaf (fragrant, herbal)

Over 90% of British blackcurrants go into making squash (fruit cordial) (Ribena, we need to have words), which I confess makes it kind of annoying to source blackcurrants for this cake. Still, the truth is this: blackcurrants are wasted in squash and you really ought to make this cake. This is one of those easy-going, rustic cakes that you rustle up in a random afternoon, just because. But it's also a total knockout: the tangy tartness of blackcurrants is the perfect foil to the plush richness that the clotted cream contributes to the batter, and the fragrance of bay provides additional dimension. Probably one of the best things I've ever made or tasted.

Serves 8-10

for the cake
100g (3½oz) salted butter,
    plus extra for greasing
5-7 bay leaves, depending on size
2 eggs
1 x 227g (8oz) pot of clotted cream
200g (7oz/1 cup) granulated sugar
200g (7oz/1½ cups plus 1 tbsp)
    self-raising flour
½ tsp fine sea salt
¼ tsp baking powder
¼ tsp bicarbonate of soda
    (baking soda)
50g (2oz) blackcurrants, frozen/fresh
    (off the stem)/tinned
1 tbsp demerara
    (turbinado) sugar

for the compote
250g (9oz) blackcurrants, frozen
    or fresh (off the stem)
3 tbsp caster (superfine) sugar
3 bay leaves

equipment
20cm (8in) non-stick springform
    cake tin

1   Melt the butter along with two of the bay leaves, broken in half, then set aside to cool slightly (remove the bay leaves just before using).

2   Preheat the oven to 160°C fan/180°C/350°F/gas 4. Grease the tin and line the base with greaseproof paper.

3   For the compote, place all the ingredients in a medium saucepan along with a tablespoon of water. Bring to a simmer over a medium-high heat and cook until the blackcurrants deflate and the compote thickens and becomes a little jammy, around 4 minutes. Set aside to cool, removing the bay leaves before using.

4   For the cake, whisk together the eggs and clotted cream until there are no large lumps. Whisk in the granulated sugar, beating the mix for a minute or so (as if you were whipping cream) in order to incorporate some air into the batter.

5   Sift the dry ingredients together into a medium bowl, then sift (again) directly into the clotted cream mix. Whisk until just incorporated, then stir through the melted butter.

6   Spoon half of the batter into the lined tin, then spoon over the blackcurrant compote. Dollop the remaining batter evenly over the top of the compote, then use an offset spatula (or the back of a spoon) to spread it evenly (try to get the cake batter to cover the blackcurrant compote, but don't worry if it swirls together a bit). Scatter over the blackcurrants, followed by the demerara sugar, then slip the additional bay leaves into the top of the cake.

7   Bake until golden and an inserted skewer comes out clean, around 50–55 minutes. Allow to cool for 5 minutes before running a knife around the edges and releasing from the tin. Serve warm or once cooled – both delicious!

bee sting cake (bienenstich)

The sponge ensures a deeper flavour, as well a loaf that will retain its moisture for longer.

This is best served within an hour or so of being assembled.

Since the brioche needs to hang out in the fridge overnight, I make the pastry cream, dough and syrup on day 1, then finish, bake and assemble the cake on day 2 – although it's worth knowing that the pastry cream and syrup could be made up to 3 days ahead.

balancing elements
yeast (fermented/umami)
almond crunch topping (subtly bitter)
salt

The German cake bienenstich, 'bee sting cake', might well have the most charming name of any cake. A bit like a French tropezienne, it's a yeasted, enriched dough that is split and filled with pastry cream. But the key – and important – difference between the two is the addictive, crunchy, honey-almond topping that's baked into the top of this one, for the stories say that this is what attracted the bees.

Serves around 10

for the sponge
60ml (2¼fl oz/¼ cup) whole milk
1 tsp caster (superfine) sugar
6g (¼oz/1 sachet) active dry yeast
  (I use Borwick's)
60g (2¼oz/½ cup) plain
  (all-purpose) flour
  (min. 11% protein)

for the dough
300g (10½oz/scant 2½ cups)
  plain (all-purpose) flour
50g (2oz/¼ cup) caster
  (superfine) sugar
¾ tsp fine sea salt
zest of 1 orange
3 large eggs, at room temperature
100g (3½oz) butter, at room
  temperature, plus
  extra for greasing
1 egg, beaten, for egg wash

1 Start by making the sponge. Add the milk and sugar to a small saucepan and place over a low-medium heat for around a minute, giving it the occasional stir, until it's warm to touch (no more than 35°C/95°F). Transfer to the bowl of the stand mixer and, by hand, mix in the yeast and flour until you have a thick dough. Cover and place somewhere warm for 1–1½ hours. It will have developed a holey texture and should smell quite yeasty (fermented, beery, slightly acidic).

2 Add the flour, sugar, salt, orange zest and eggs to the sponge, then mix in the stand mixer for around 12–14 minutes, occasionally pausing to scrape down the sides. After this time, the dough should have pulled away from the sides and be forming more of a ball around the dough hook. With the mixer still running, add the butter a tablespoon at a time – you want each tablespoon to have been incorporated before you add the next. Adding the butter will take you around 10–15 minutes, and the dough should become shiny, soft, stretchy and not too sticky. Allow the mixer to run until you can successfully carry out the windowpane test (where you can pull apart a thin, almost translucent layer of the dough with your fingers, see page 52), another 10 minutes or so. Cover the bowl with cling film (plastic wrap) and leave to prove until it's almost doubled in size, around 1 hour (see tip on next page). Knock the air out of the dough then re-cover and transfer to the fridge to rest overnight.

3 Grease your springform tin and place a circle of greaseproof paper in the base. Lightly knead the dough, then transfer it to the tin, pressing it gently into a round to cover the base. Cover lightly with cling film (plastic wrap) and leave to prove until puffy (when a finger is pushed into the dough it springs back slowly but not completely), around 1–2 hours. Towards the end of this time, preheat the oven to 170°C fan/190°C/375°F/gas 5 and place a baking tray in the oven to heat up at the same time. (If you have been proving your dough in the oven, remove it before preheating.)

Recipe and ingredients continue overleaf

for the almond crunch topping

70g (2¾oz) butter
40g (1½oz/3 heaped tbsp)
    caster (superfine) sugar
3 tbsp runny honey
2 tbsp double (heavy) cream
large pinch of flaky sea salt
100g (3½oz) flaked almonds

for the pastry cream

500ml (17fl oz/generous 2 cups)
    whole milk
120g (4½oz/scant 1 cup) caster
    (superfine) sugar
2 tsp vanilla bean paste
6 large egg yolks
45g (1¾oz/2 heaped tbsp)
    cornflour (cornstarch)

for the orange blossom syrup

40g (1½oz/1½ tbsp) runny honey
50ml (2fl oz/3 tbsp plus 1 tsp) water
1½ tsp orange blossom water
    (I use the Cortas brand)

equipment

temperature probe
    (helpful, not essential)
stand mixer fitted with a dough hook
23cm (9in) non-stick, springform
    cake tin (or similar)
piping bag (helpful, not essential)

4   Meanwhile, make the almond crunch topping. Add all the ingredients except the flaked almonds to a small saucepan and place over a low heat until everything is melted. Increase the heat and bring to a light simmer, allowing it to bubble away until it turns a shade darker, around 3 minutes. Remove from the heat and stir in the flaked almonds, then set aside to cool.

5   To make the pastry cream, add the milk, half of the sugar (eyeball this) and the vanilla to a small saucepan and heat until the milk is steaming. Separately, add the egg yolks, the remaining sugar and cornflour to a bowl and whisk together until light and fluffy, 1–2 minutes. Whisk a third of the milk mixture into the eggs, then pour the egg mixture into the pan with the rest of the milk and whisk together to combine. Cook the custard, whisking continuously until it thickens considerably, between 5 and 10 minutes (it will seem like nothing's happening for a while, but then it will thicken quickly). Transfer to a container, cover the surface with cling film (plastic wrap) and set aside to cool completely (if you're concerned about lumps in your custard then you can strain it before leaving it to cool).

6   For the orange blossom syrup, add the honey, water and orange blossom water to your smallest saucepan and set over a low heat until the honey has melted. Increase the heat and simmer until the mixture has thickened slightly, around 2–3 minutes, then set aside.

7   Once the dough has proved, brush it with the egg wash, then dollop the almond crunch on top (it should almost cover the dough). Bake on the preheated tray until the cake is risen and bronzed, around 20–25 minutes. Allow to cool in the tin for around 5 minutes before running a knife gently around the edges and releasing the cake from the tin. Allow to cool completely.

8   To put it all together, slice the cake into 2 layers (like a giant burger bun) – I like to cut it two-thirds of the way up, so that the top is slightly lighter and doesn't squash the pastry cream too much. Brush both cut sides with the orange blossom syrup. Briefly whisk the pastry cream to loosen it up, then transfer it to a piping bag and pipe the cream onto the base layer of the cake (or simply spoon it on). Top with the other half of the cake, pushing down slightly. Best served within an hour or so.

Tip A great way to create a reliable environment to prove doughs is to turn your oven on for exactly 60 seconds, then turn it off – this will create the perfect warm environment. See also: Rum + Grapefruit Babas (page 46) and Cardamom Brioche Loaf (page 50).

no-churn dulce de leche ice cream

The dulce de leche can be made in advance and stored for up to a week in the fridge.

Serve scoops of this topped with salted popcorn.

The inclusion of dark rum helps the ice cream stay a softer, more scoopable texture, but it can be left out if you cannot consume alcohol.

balancing elements
rum (bitter)
salt

It would have been a gross oversight to create this chapter and fail to include dulce de leche, which translates as 'jam of milk'. And while I know some of us might be familiar with the whole boil-a-can-of-condensed-milk approach to this South American delight, I'm going to suggest that we transition to the real deal – are you with me?

I should say upfront that making dulce de leche from scratch requires no additional time – just a little mindful attention – and every minute of that focus is rewarded, in the end, with unrivalled depth of flavour. Plus, once you've invested in homemade dulce de leche as the base of your ice cream, it's easy from there on in: you simply whip it up with double (heavy) cream and freeze.

Makes around 1 litre

for the dulce de leche
1½ litres (2½ pints) whole milk
75ml (2¾fl oz/⅓ cup) double (heavy) cream
240g (8¾oz/scant 1¼ cups) granulated sugar
¼ tsp cream of tartar, plus an extra pinch
¼ tsp bicarbonate of soda (baking soda), plus an extra pinch

for the ice cream
375g (13oz) dulce de leche (see above)
500ml (17fl oz/generous 2 cups) double (heavy) cream, fridge-cold
2 tbsp dark rum
1 tsp flaky sea salt
salted popcorn, to serve

equipment
900g (2lb) loaf tin
electric hand whisk

1 Start with the dulce de leche. Add the milk, cream and sugar to a heavy-based saucepan and set over a medium heat, stirring occasionally until the sugar has dissolved, around 10 minutes. Scoop out an espresso-cup's-worth of the liquid. Whisk the cream of tartar and bicarb into this, before whisking the mixture back into the pan (use a spatula to make sure you don't leave any of the mix behind). Turn the heat up and bring to a brisk simmer, stirring occasionally to make sure nothing is sticking to the bottom of the pan (the mix will look foamy – this is normal). Cook until it turns a pale creamy tan colour, around 1 hour. From this point, stir the mixture frequently with a whisk as it darkens and thickens, until you have a medium tan colour, around 30 minutes. Strain through a sieve into a container (it may still be quite liquid but it will thicken) and place aside (if it happens to be a little grainy you can run a stick blender through it once it has cooled). Once fully cool, it can be sealed and stored in the fridge until needed.

2 Line your loaf tin with cling film (plastic wrap) so that there is a decent overhang on each side (both to cover the top of the ice cream and to act as a sling if you should want to remove it later).

3 To make the no-churn ice cream, add 375g (13oz) of the dulce de leche to a bowl (any left over can be drizzled over cakes, used as a filling for biscuits or served with churros) and incorporate half of the cream with an electric whisk to loosen up the caramel. Add the rest of the cream and whisk until soft peaks forms. Finally, whisk in the rum and salt. Pour the mixture into the lined loaf tin, cover with the cling film and freeze for at least 4–6 hours, or overnight.

4 To serve, scoop balls of the ice cream into bowls and top with salted popcorn.

Tip Adding alcohol to ice creams not only adds flavour, it also inhibits crystallisation – resulting in a smoother ice cream. See also: The Neo Neapolitan (page 88).

russian honey (crêpe) cake

This is best made a few hours before you want to serve (or it's even better after an overnight stint in the fridge).

For speed and ease, you could opt to use store-bought crêpes and caramel sauce.

The filling can be made the day before – simply store in a sealed container in the fridge and bring to room temperature before using (you can loosen it, if needed, with a splash of milk).

balancing elements
sour cream (sour/tangy)
cream cheese (sour/tangy)
burnt honey (subtly bitter)

Russian honey cake is made with a gazillion skinny layers of a sponge-biscuit hybrid, which is how I came to settle on the idea of this crêpe cake – an altogether quicker prospect. Here's what we appreciate about crêpe cakes: they're straightforward to make (no baking!); they feel indulgent while also being light; and they look impressive. In short, they're a fun option for a celebratory occasion.

Serves 10

for the crêpes
3 eggs
75g (3oz/generous ⅓ cup) caster (superfine) sugar
500ml (17fl oz/generous 2 cups) whole milk
250g (9oz/2 cups) plain (all-purpose) flour
1 tsp ground ginger
½ tsp ground cinnamon
½ tsp mixed spice
½ tsp fine sea salt
20g (¾oz) butter, melted, plus extra for cooking

for the burnt honey filling
110g (4oz/generous ¼ cup) runny honey
220ml (7½fl oz/scant 1 cup) sour cream
2 x 165g (5½oz) packs of full-fat cream cheese

for the caramel sauce
60g (2½oz/⅓ cup) soft light brown (or light muscovado) sugar
15g (½oz) butter, at room temperature
120ml (4fl oz/½ cup) double (heavy) cream
½ tsp vanilla bean paste
¼ tsp flaky sea salt, or to taste
40g (1½oz) blanched hazelnuts, toasted and lightly crushed

equipment
20cm (8in) crêpe pan (or frying pan/skillet)

1   Make the crêpe batter by whisking together the eggs and caster sugar, along with 100ml (3½floz/generous ⅓ cup) of the milk. Whisk in the flour, spices and salt, but don't worry about lumps. Gradually add the rest of the milk, incorporating it a third at a time until you have a fairly liquid batter. Stir through the melted butter, then sieve the batter to get rid of any lumps and set aside to rest.

2   For the filling, put the honey into a small, light-coloured saucepan and simmer over a medium heat until it turns several shades darker, around 7–10 minutes (take it off the heat if it starts to smoke). Slowly whisk in the sour cream and set aside. Separately, whisk the cream cheese until smooth, then whisk in the honey-sour cream mixture. Cover and place in the fridge to chill.

3   Heat a crêpe pan or frying pan (skillet) to a medium-high heat. Add a little knob of butter and allow it to melt, then use some kitchen paper to wipe it around the pan to grease. Pour 50ml (2fl oz/3 tbsp plus 1 tsp) of the batter into the pan, tilting it to ensure an even crêpe. It should take no more than a minute or so for the underside to take on a golden colour. Flip it and allow to cook on the second side for 30 seconds, then transfer to a plate. Repeat with the remaining batter, greasing as necessary and stacking the pancakes up on the plate (they shouldn't stick). Allow them to cool completely. You should get around 16–18 crêpes.

4   To assemble, lay a crêpe on your serving plate and spread with 2–3 tablespoons of the filling (or 40g/1½oz, to be precise). Repeat until you've used up all the filling, leaving the crêpe on top unadorned.

5   To make the caramel sauce, combine the light brown sugar and butter in a heavy-based saucepan and set over a medium-high heat. Bring to a simmer, then reduce the heat and let it bubble away until you've reached the desired colour (I like a deep toffee colour), around 10 minutes. Turn the heat down to low, add the cream and cook the sauce for a minute or so. Stir in the vanilla and salt, then the hazelnuts. Immediately pour over the stack of filled crêpes, nudging the sauce to the edges with your spoon. Place in the fridge to chill for 2–3 hours before serving.

Tip Most batters – whether for Yorkshire puddings, crêpes, blinis, etc. – benefit from some resting time before cooking, as this allows the flour to properly absorb the liquid. See also: Crêpes with Plantain + Rum Caramel (page 68).

pears

breakfast croissant pudding with anise pears **175**

brown butter, pear + hazelnut cake **176**

fierce ginger, pear + pepper cake **178**

chocolate + pear self-saucing pudding **179**

salted buttermilk pudding + roasted pears **180**

pear + acv tarte tatin **182**

pear sorbet with frozen roquefort **186**

Confession: in the past I've struggled to find space in my heart for pears. Many love their floral aroma and unique texture and they are the fruit that perhaps most screams 'autumn!' – but I have a problem with them. I have a problem with pears and it's their lack of acidity. Apples and pears have similar levels of sugar but, on average, apples have 0.8% acidity while pears have 0.2%. That seemingly tiny 0.6% differential changes *everything*: it's the reason that pears register as much sweeter on our palates. As Harold McGee, author of the seminal *On Food and Cooking*, puts it: 'the sweeter a fruit is, the tastier it is, but even a sweet fruit will seem one-dimensional without some counterbalancing acidity.' Which gets to the crux of the matter: for me, in spite of their aromatic qualities, pears often lack dimension. Until now, I have been resolutely and unwaveringly an apple girl. But, Reader, I wrote this chapter and I changed my mind.

The pear has been the work of centuries. Originally hard-fleshed and very gritty, breeders in France and the surrounding regions gradually reduced these qualities over the eighteenth century, resulting in the softer, buttery texture we associate with the fruit today. Likewise, in the process of developing this chapter I have considerably softened towards the pear, coming to appreciate what it has to offer in the realm of desserts (and beyond). It turns out that the acidity that makes apples so delicious is precisely what gets in the way of them pairing readily with other flavours. Sure, apples work well with spices and nuts, but apple desserts and bakes tend to be a single-fruit affair: apple turnover, tarte Tatin, apple pie, *tarte aux pommes*, Eve's pudding, apple Charlotte, baked apples – apples tend to be a solo act, a monologue. Pears, on the other hand, pair beautifully with several ingredients: bitter and tannic flavours like dark chocolate (see page 179), red wine, beer and molasses; dairy products, from the fresh tang of yoghurt to the sharp, umami of Parmesan and blue cheese (see page 186); tart berries such as cranberries and blackberries (I would be remiss if I didn't direct you to the utterly delicious pear and cranberry pie in my previous cookbook, *Bitter*); and all manner of nuts and spices. The humble pear, it turns out, is a real team player.

The pear's other USP is its supremely elegant drop-like form, which I suspect plays a considerable part in the popularity of a poached pear (a dessert that can be conveniently taken in any number of flavour directions). Some classic options are pears poached in red wine, or Poires Belle-Hélène: a majestic poached pear served with rich chocolate sauce and Chantilly. Created by renowned French chef Escoffier in Paris in the 1860s, it was inspired by the soprano

Hortense Schneider, who was starring in a musical parody, *La Belle Hélène*. The show was a flamboyant affair (frenzied songs, flashy costumes), and the story goes that Hortense seduced Escoffier, who was working at nearby restaurant Le Petit Moulin Rouge at the time. (Escoffier seems to have had a thing for sopranos, as he also created the Peach Melba 30 years later, for the Australian soprano Nellie Melba, see page 102.) What Escoffier intimately understood was that sweetness is nothing without a counterpart – that a perfectly sweet, milky-white poached pear would sing alongside something darker and more bitter. Needless to say, pears and chocolate are one of the most perfect matches.

While pears are available year-round, they are most associated with autumn (fall) and winter – in part due to their flavour bedfellows (warming spices, caramel, chocolate, etc.). The most common variety in the UK is the Conference pear: tall, thin, a little gritty and a reliable all-rounder, it works well both raw and cooked. If you like this sort of texture, then Bosc pears are another option. Texturally, I prefer the buttery quality of Comice, Anjou, Beurre Hardy (the picture book pear!) and Rocha; but my ultimate favourite is the Williams pear (known as Bartlett in the States). Williams pears are used to make eau de vie Poire William – a process which sees the pears fermented, then distilled into a bright, fresh pear brandy – and they are the most tart of all the pears, which naturally recommends them to me. They're excellent raw and beautiful in a sorbet (see page 186), but sadly have their limitations when cooked, since they quickly fall apart. Beyond the more common varieties, there are blush pears, Winter Nellis, Decana and several hundred others, some of which are expressly used to make perry (cider made with pears). The Asian Nashi pear, meanwhile, is practically a different fruit: shaped like an apple, and with a similarly crisp texture, it is best served raw.

Generally, a ripe pear – no matter the type – should give a little when pressed lightly around the stem end. But whatever you do, take care to avoid pears that are too soft as they don't take much encouragement to fall apart . . . and the beauty of a pear, after all, is in its refined, feminine shape.

breakfast croissant pudding with anise pears

Stale bakery croissants are fantastic in this, but supermarket versions work too – just make sure they're all-butter.

If possible, allow the croissants to soak overnight (ideal for a weekend brunch!) – otherwise go ahead and bake it immediately.

To make this coeliac-friendly, use gluten-free croissants.

I get best results in a deep baking dish (e.g. Falcon Enamelware 30cm/12in rectangular pie dish) but you can use something shallower if that's what you have.

balancing elements
extra-virgin olive oil (bitter)
sherry (bitter)
light muscovado (subtle acidity)
fennel seeds (herbal, subtly bitter)
salt

Serves 4–6

25g (1oz) butter, plus extra
   for greasing
25ml (1fl oz) extra-virgin olive oil
50g (2oz/¼ cup) light muscovado
   (or light brown) sugar
2 tbsp runny honey
¾ tsp flaky sea salt (I use Maldon)
4 eggs
300ml (10fl oz/1⅓ cups) whole milk
2 tsp vanilla bean paste
2 tbsp dry sherry (optional)
3–4 stale, all-butter croissants
1 tbsp demerara (turbinado) sugar
1 tsp ground cinnamon
Greek yoghurt, to serve (optional)

for the pears
20g (¾oz) butter
2 tbsp maple syrup
1 tsp anise (or fennel) seeds,
   lightly crushed
1½ tsp apple cider vinegar
4 medium pears (any type, just ripe),
   peeled, halved and cored

equipment
baking dish to snugly fit the croissants
baking dish to snugly fit the pears

Inspired by Spanish torrijas, this is made easy for serving a crowd by baking in a single dish. The extra-virgin olive oil, sherry, fennel seeds and sea salt offer a savoury edge that cuts through the buttery croissants and sweet pears . . . possibly my favourite recipe in the book!

1   Melt the 25g (1oz) of butter in a small saucepan over a low heat, then stir in the olive oil, sugar, honey and salt. Heat through until the sugar has dissolved and the mixture has thickened. Pour into the base of the greased baking dish, spreading to the edges, then set aside.

2   Next, make the custard. Whisk the eggs, milk, vanilla and sherry, if using (I recommend it!), together in a wide bowl. Halve the croissants laterally, as if you were making a sandwich, then dip the bases into the egg mix and arrange them across the base of the baking dish. Repeat with the tops, placing them on top of each base, (essentially putting the croissant back together again). Pour over any remaining custard and gently push the croissants down so that they are partly submerged. Cover and leave to soak in the fridge – ideally overnight, or for 15 minutes if you'd like to cook this immediately.

3   When ready to bake, preheat the oven to 160°C fan/180°C/350°F/gas 4.

4   For the pears, add the butter, maple syrup, anise (or fennel) seeds and vinegar to a baking dish and place in the oven for a couple of minutes until melted. Remove from the oven and add the pears, cut-sides down, then turn them over so that they're coated in the butter-syrup mix.

5   Sprinkle the top of the croissants with the demerara sugar and ground cinnamon, then place in the oven along with the pears on the shelf above. Bake until the pears are tender (turn them over halfway through cooking) and the croissants are puffed and golden, about 30 minutes. Allow both to cool for 5 minutes before eating with Greek yoghurt, if liked.

brown butter, pear + hazelnut cake

If you don't have a food processor, simply replace the hazelnuts with store-bought ground almonds.

Make this coeliac-friendly by replacing the flour with gluten-free flour.

You can also cook this in a 23cm (9in) pan – the pears will just sink into the cake more.

Best served with crème fraîche to cut through the richness of the brown butter and sweetness of the pears.

balancing elements
lemon juice (sour)
lemon zest (bitter)
hazelnuts (subtly bitter)
brown butter (subtle umami)

Financiers – little French almond cakes made with browned butter – are severely underrated: they're delicious, quick to make, easily made gluten free and a fantastic use of leftover egg whites. Enter this large version, adapted from Alison Roman: I use pears in lieu of her torn plums, and hazelnuts instead of the more classic almonds, but essentially this is one of those versatile cakes where apricots and almonds, or raspberries and pistachios would also work beautifully.

Serves 8-10

75g (3oz) blanched hazelnuts; plus 25g (1oz), lightly crushed, for the top
180g (6oz) butter
90g (3¼oz) runny honey
2 medium pears (any type), around 280g (10oz)
juice and zest of 1 lemon
75g (3oz/⅔ cup) plain (all-purpose) flour
140g (3¾oz/scant 1½ cups) icing (confectioners') sugar, sifted
¼ tsp fine sea salt
5 egg whites
2 tbsp demerara (turbinado) sugar

equipment
20cm (8in) sandwich cake tin, at least 3cm (1in) deep
food processor

1 Preheat the oven to 180°C fan/200°C/400°F/gas 6. Push a large piece of greaseproof paper into the cake tin (it'll look rustic!).

2 Pulse the 75g (3oz) hazelnuts in the food processor until just slightly coarser than ground almonds. Be careful not to process them too much or else you'll end up with nut butter (delicious, but not what we're after here).

3 Separately, brown the butter in a pan over a medium heat, taking it as far as you can without burning it – this usually takes 10–15 minutes. Allow to cool for 5–10 minutes before whisking in the honey.

4 Prepare the pears. Squeeze the lemon juice into a medium bowl. Peel, core and chop your pears, adding the pieces to the bowl and tossing to coat as you go (the lemon juice stops them going brown).

5 To make the cake, whisk together the flour, icing sugar, salt, ground hazelnuts and lemon zest in a medium–large bowl. In a separate bowl, whisk together the egg whites until frothy. Pour the egg whites into the dry ingredients and whisk until smooth and homogenous (but no longer!). Next, whisk in the melted butter mixture, then pour the batter into the prepared cake tin (it will be quite full, but don't panic as this cake doesn't rise much).

6 Drop the pear pieces into the batter and sprinkle over the lightly crushed hazelnuts and demerara sugar. Bake in the oven for 40 minutes, turning the tin halfway through. The cake should be golden with darker edges, but still a little wet in the middle (the pears will add a lot of moisture, so it'll be easy to think that the batter isn't cooked, when in fact it is). Allow to cool for 5–10 minutes before slicing.

Tip Demerara (turbinado) sugar adds essential crunchy texture (and a sparkly effect) to the top of this cake – a trick worth using across any rustic bakes. See also: Blackcurrant, Bay + Clotted Cream Cake (page 163), Black Tea Eccles Cakes (page 196), Raspberry + Coconut Hand Pies (page 116) and Breakfast Croissant Pudding with Anise Pears (page 175).

pear + acv tarte tatin

I was going for 'the perfect tarte Tatin' with this recipe, so although there are a few extra steps (e.g. drying the pears out in the fridge overnight, two different pans, etc.) I promise it's for good reason.

The caramel can be made up to a week in advance and stored in an airtight container in the fridge, then gently rewarmed.

The tart can be constructed and stored in the fridge for a day or so before baking (just make sure all the components are cold before you put it together).

Best served with crème fraîche.

balancing elements
apple cider vinegar (sour)
dark caramel (bitter/sweet)
salt

There's a reason that apple tarte Tatin is a classic, and it's because apples have sufficient acidity to counterbalance all that caramel and butter. Pears bring many things to the table (a floral quality and buttery flesh) but acidity is not one of them, which is why I have made this caramel with apple cider vinegar and suggested you take it reasonably far: it's intentionally a bit bitter, a bit sour and a bit salty – the pears demand it because they're very sweet and need some challenge.

Serves 4–6

for the pears
5–6 large Conference or Concorde pears (around 700–800g/ 1lb 9oz–1lb 12oz total weight), relatively hard

for the ACV caramel
45g (1½oz) butter, fridge-cold and cubed
110ml (3¾fl oz/scant ½ cup) double (heavy) cream
1½ tsp flaky sea salt
3 tbsp apple cider vinegar
300g (10½oz/1½ cups) caster (superfine) or granulated sugar

to assemble
1 sheet of all-butter ready-rolled puff pastry (I highly recommend Dorset Pastry)
crème fraîche, to serve

equipment
large metal frying pan (skillet) for cooking the pears
20cm (8in) ovenproof frying pan (skillet) for assembling the tarte

1 Peel, halve and core your pears, then lay them out on a tray lined with kitchen paper. Place in the fridge for a minimum of 6 hours (overnight is ideal/easiest; 2 days is even better!).

2 Next, make the caramel. Before you start, place your cold butter, double cream, salt and 1 tablespoon of the apple cider vinegar by the stove, all measured out. Place your large metal frying pan over a medium heat and sprinkle over some of the sugar in a thin layer. Allow this to start to melt and turn golden – you can give it an occasional stir with a heatproof spatula – then sprinkle over another thin layer and, again, allow it to melt. Repeat until all the sugar has been used up, then cook the caramel until it turns a deep amber colour, becomes very fluid (there shouldn't be any un-melted grains of sugar) and releases light wisps of smoke. Once you've taken the caramel as far are you dare, take it off the heat and whisk in the butter, followed by the cream, the tablespoon of vinegar and the salt. It may seize up but keep whisking and it'll melt back into a fluid sauce. Use your heatproof spatula to make sure everything is well incorporated. Being very careful, gently pour around 125ml (4¼fl oz/½ cup) of the caramel into a measuring jug and set aside, leaving the rest in the frying pan.

3 Add the remaining 2 tablespoons of vinegar to the caramel left in the pan, then add the pears (don't worry if they don't all fit initially – they will shrink as they cook). Place over a medium heat and bring the caramel to a light simmer. Cook the pears until softened but not falling apart, around 10 minutes (flipping the pears halfway through). Switch off the heat and allow the pears to cool in the caramel.

4   Meanwhile, prepare your pastry by cutting out a circle that is just slightly bigger than the diameter of your 20cm (8in) frying pan. Working around the circumference, fold 1cm (½in) of the dough over itself, pinching down firmly, to create a small rim at the edge of the pastry. Poke the pastry all over with a fork, then return to the fridge until ready to use.

5   Pour the reserved caramel into the 20cm (8in) frying pan (this is the one you will compile the tarte in).

6   Preheat the oven to 220°C fan/240°C/475°F/gas 9.

7   Drain the pears from the caramel they've been cooking in (the leftover caramel can be strained and used to glaze the tart once you've turned it out – or be saved for serving with ice cream). Arrange the pears in the pan in a circle, rounded-sides down, stem-ends facing into the centre. Make sure you fit as many pears in as you can, you want it to be quite crowded. (If you've used a more rounded pear such as Comice, there might be a gap in the middle to be filled with another pear half.) Place the pastry on top of the pears, using a spoon to help you tuck it in around the edges. Use a paring knife to slice a couple of vents into the centre of the pastry. (At this point, you can bake the tarte Tatin immediately or place it in the fridge to bake later.)

8   Bake the tarte Tatin for 15 minutes until the pastry is risen and has started to turn golden, then turn the oven down to 160°C fan/180°C/350°F/gas 4 and cook for a further 20 minutes, then turn the heat down again to 120°C fan/140°C/275°F/gas 1 and cook for another 30 minutes. Remove the pan from the oven and set aside to cool for a minimum of 30 minutes or up to 1 hour.

9   To invert the tart, work over the sink and place a wire cooling rack over the pan. Hold the two firmly together and then in one swift movement invert the tart, allowing any excess juices to flow off into the sink. Transfer the tart from the wire rack to a plate. Glaze with the extra caramel (if liked), then serve slices with a big dollop of crème fraîche.

Tip When it comes to baking anything with pie dough (or puff pastry), it always needs a lot longer in the oven than you think it will. You'll be tempted to remove this tart halfway through the cooking time because it'll seemingly look 'done', but you'll be rewarded if you hold out. See also: Peach Melba Galette (page 102), Raspberry + Coconut Hand Pies (page 116) and Black Tea Eccles Cakes (page 196).

pear
sorbet
with frozen
roquefort

If you can, use a mix of pear varieties – I would recommend throwing in some Williams pears for acidity.

If you can, chill the mixture overnight in the fridge before churning.

This sorbet is ideally eaten within a couple of days, when its texture is best.

If you leave off the cheese, this sorbet is vegan and gluten-free.

balancing elements
Roquefort (salty/umami)
lemon juice (sour)
vodka (bitter)

**Makes around 750ml
(1¼ pints) sorbet
(8–10 scoops)**

for the sorbet
190ml (6¾fl oz/generous ¾ cup) filtered water
40ml (1¼fl oz/2 tbsp plus 2 tsp) fresh lemon juice
800g (1lb 12oz) pears
90g (3¼oz/scant ½ cup) caster (superfine) sugar
1½ tbsp vodka (optional)

for the frozen Roquefort
100g (3½oz) Roquefort

equipment
stick blender (or standard blender)
ice cream maker

If you like to finish a meal with cheese, then this is the dessert for you. And if you don't? Well, the frozen Roquefort is entirely optional – which is to say: this is an excellent pear sorbet!

1   Start with the frozen Roquefort. Remove any rind, then crumble it into small to medium pieces into a Tupperware box. Freeze for at least 4 hours. After this time, blend the frozen Roquefort in small batches in a food processor until more finely crumbled. Freeze again. After a couple of hours you should have crumbled frozen blue cheese, ready to use whenever you need.

2   To make the sorbet, add the water and lemon juice to a large saucepan, then peel, core and chop the pears into 2–3cm (1in) pieces, adding them to the water as you go (this will stop them oxidising). Cover and bring to a gentle simmer, cooking until the pears are tender, around 15 minutes. Remove from the heat.

3   Add the sugar and vodka (if using) to the pan, then blend until smooth with a stick blender (alternatively, transfer to a counter-top blender). Pass the mix through a sieve, then store in a sealed container in the fridge to chill overnight (or you can go ahead and churn it immediately once it's fully cooled). Churn the sorbet according to your machine's instructions.

4   To serve, top a scoop of pear sorbet with a scattering of the frozen Roquefort.

Tip Vodka is a useful ingredient in cooking: it inhibits gluten formation in batters and doughs where you want to preserve lightness/flakiness; it inhibits crystallisation in ice creams and sorbets (which is its purpose in this recipe); and it also carries flavour (hence why penne alla vodka is so well-loved!). See also: No-Churn Dulce de Leche Ice Cream, which uses rum for the same purpose (page 167).

dates +
dried fruit

During Ramadan, Muslims fast from sunrise to sunset. When it comes time to break this fast, the best option – as espoused by the prophet Muhammed – is to start with dates, which quickly replenish the body's reserves. In the holy city of Mecca, when it's time to break the fast and just before the call to prayer, the Guard open the gates and truck after truck streams through. No one knows exactly who has sent them – though it's fair to assume they come from the most affluent – but the contents are familiar to Muslims: packets upon packets of the freshest dates as a gift from Allah. The crowds do not shove or push – there'll be enough for everyone – instead they wait patiently for a packet to land in their palms. This image, shared with me by my fellow MasterChef finalist Madeeha, perfectly illustrates that to understand dates, you must understand the significance of the date palm across the Middle East and Africa, and for Muslims around the world.

Before the Middle East was mined for its oil, it was simply a sweltering, arid area with temperatures that could exceed 50°C (120°F). Those who survived lived a nomadic, Bedouin lifestyle and, in the absence of much else to sustain them, were heavily dependent on the date palm – one of the only trees to thrive in the burning heat of the desert (scientists call it the 'phoenix'). The dates served as food (a single palm can produce 50kg/110lb of fruit per year, for several decades) and a natural sweetener, while the leaves offered building materials and shelter for other crops. In short, the date palm almost single-handedly kept people alive. It comes as no surprise, then, that Muslims include dates in all major life events and holy days; they are present at birth (a child's first taste is a tiny quantity of the fruit, a practice called *tahneek*), marriage *and* death. Madeeha told me that one of her most treasured memories is of her late father administering *tahneek* to her eldest son.

While dates in the Middle East might commonly be eaten fresh, those that arrive at other locations in the world, including the UK, are dried. The practice of drying fruits seems to have started, predictably, where the sun is strongest: the earliest recorded mention is from Mesopotamian tablets dating around 1700 BC. It was a process that would have started organically: figs or plums falling off the tree, lying on the ground in the hot sun, the water gradually evaporating, leaving behind edible jewels. But eventually humans started to carry out the process more intentionally. By definition, dried fruits have a lower water content than fresh fruit, which means a more concentrated flavour (and sweetness), as well as the ability to store them for months. Raisins remain the global bestseller, but dates trail closely behind, followed by prunes, figs and apricots.

A date – sticky, resiny, fudgy, chewy – is a concentrated nugget of sweetness, nutrients and energy: if strawberries are Mother Nature's candy (see page 74), then dates are her toffee. Eat a pecan stuffed into the middle of a Medjool date and you could easily imagine that you were eating a piece of pecan pie. But in spite of their indulgent, caramel-like flavour, dates deliver all sorts of vitamins (A, B complex) and minerals (magnesium, iron, phosphorous, copper, calcium, potassium) that support healthy body tissue and muscles. Traditional desserts involving dates include British sticky toffee pudding, of course, but in the Middle East it's baked goods such as *maamoul*, a semolina-based pastry dough stuffed with a spiced date paste.

Dried fruits – at least the kind common in the UK (raisins, sultanas/golden raisins, currants) – seem to have fallen out of favour in recent years (the downward trend for the traditional Christmas pudding is a key indicator), but I remain a fan. I suspect this appreciation was born at my grandmother's table through her traditional British cooking (her mince pies? Still the best ever). But I also fondly remember being allowed to choose little bags of dried fruit, pick 'n' mix style, from the French supermarkets when young – sweet enough to satisfy a craving and satisfyingly chewy: who needed Haribo?

I use various dried fruit in this chapter, from raisins to dried figs to cranberries, but can I also make a case for the humble prune? Beyond being high in fibre, prunes are particularly delicious because the plums they're created from have naturally high acidity, which results in something neither too sweet nor too sour. Plus their larger size (vs the grapes that then become raisins) ensures they stay jammy, rather than drying out too much. Regardless of type, dried fruits have many uses: as fillings for mince pies and Eccles cakes (page 196), in sponges and fruit cakes (page 203), in tagines and curries to add sweetness and tang, and as a way of punctuating pilafs and salads. And the true beauty of dried fruit is the fact that it eschews the seasons, offering fruity sweetness year-round, including the barren winter months. They are little jewels in your kitchen cupboard – and they ought to be treasured.

currant dutch baby with honeyed ricotta

For the best result, ensure the majority of your ingredients are at room temperature.

Using the right size of frying pan (skillet) will help to produce that impressive pouf.

If doubling the recipe, use a 30cm (12in) pan and bear in mind that it might need a couple of extra minutes of cooking.

To make this dairy free, replace the whole milk with unsweetened coconut milk, the butter with coconut oil or a plant based spread and serve with a plant-based cream.

balancing elements
currants (sour)
lemon zest (bitter)

A Dutch Baby (aka the Lazy Person's Pancake) is a wonder. You whip up a batter, let it rest a little, pour it into a screaming hot pan and mere minutes later you're rewarded with an edible piece of art: towering, puffy, sculptural. It's one of those recipes that makes cooking feel like magic.

Serves 1-2

25g (¾oz/scant ¼ cup) currants
40g (1½oz/⅓ cup) plain
   (all-purpose) flour
1 tbsp caster (superfine)
   or granulated sugar
¼ tsp fine sea salt
zest of 1 lemon
2 eggs, at room temperature
70ml (2¾fl oz/scant ⅓ cup)
   whole milk
20g (¾oz) butter

for the honeyed ricotta
125g (4½oz) ricotta
1-2 tsp runny honey, to taste
pinch of fine sea salt
a couple of gratings of lemon zest

equipment
20cm (8in) cast-iron or ovenproof
   frying pan (skillet)

1   Place the currants in a small dish, then pour over a little boiled water to soften them.

2   Meanwhile, combine the flour, sugar, salt and lemon zest in a medium bowl, then whisk in the eggs just until the batter is smooth and lump-free. Gradually whisk in the milk, then set the batter aside to sit for 15 minutes.

3   Preheat the oven to 200°C fan/220°C/425°F/gas 7 and place the frying pan in the oven to heat up at the same time. Drain the currants of any residual liquid, and set a couple of teaspoonfuls aside to decorate.

4   Once the oven is heated and the batter has had a bit of time to rest, add the butter to the frying pan and close the oven, giving it a minute or two to melt and heat up. Open the oven (the butter should be sizzling), gently pull out the oven shelf and pour the batter into the frying pan, then sprinkle over the currants. Bake for 12–15 minutes until puffed up majestically around the edges.

5   While the Dutch baby is baking, whip together all the ingredients for the honeyed ricotta in a small bowl.

6   Remove the Dutch baby from the oven, transfer to a plate, add a spoonful of honeyed ricotta to the centre, sprinkle over the reserved currants and serve immediately.

Tip Most batters – whether for Yorkshire puddings, crêpes, blinis, farinata, etc. – benefit from some resting time before cooking. This allows the flour to properly hydrate. See also: Crêpes with Plantain + Rum Caramel (page 68), Russian Honey (Crêpe) Cake (page 168) and Far Breton (page 194).

cranberry welsh cakes

These require a 30-minute chill in the fridge prior to cooking.

A great recipe to make with kids!

balancing elements
dried cranberries (sour/subtly bitter)
lemon zest (bitter)
orange zest (subtly bitter)

Welsh cakes – stove-baked, sweetened scones/flatbreads popular in Wales – are brilliantly quick and simple sweet treats that don't require an oven. Typically they'd include raisins or currants, but I swap these out in favour of dried cranberries for their pop of bright colour and tartness. Eat them hot off the stove.

Makes around 15

225g (8oz/generous 1¾ cups)
    self-raising flour, plus extra
    for rolling out
¼ tsp fine sea salt
grated zest of ½ lemon
grated zest of ½ orange
¼ tsp grated nutmeg
100g (3½oz) cold butter,
    plus extra for cooking
50g (2oz/¼ cup) caster (superfine)
    sugar, plus extra for sprinkling
60g (2¼oz/scant ½ cup)
    dried cranberries,
    roughly chopped
1 egg beaten with 2 tbsp milk

equipment
8cm (3in) cookie cutter
large non-stick frying pan (skillet)

1   Briefly whisk together the flour, salt, citrus zests and nutmeg in a large bowl. Next, rub in the butter until the mix resembles breadcrumbs. Stir through the sugar and cranberries. Finally, add the egg and milk mixture, and stir until you have a stiff dough.

2   Turn the dough out onto a lightly floured surface and briefly knead until homogenous (don't overwork it). Roll out the dough to 5mm (¼in) thick, using extra flour, if needed.

3   Cut out the Welsh cakes using a cookie cutter, then lay them out on a lined baking tray and chill in the fridge for 30 minutes.

4   Cook the Welsh cakes in the frying pan over a medium-low heat with a little butter until golden, around 3–4 minutes each side. Sprinkle with caster sugar and eat straightaway.

far breton

This batter needs resting for an hour before cooking.

It's ideal if your ingredients are at room temperature, as this helps the batter to emulsify.

The prunes can be prepared up to a week in advance.

Delicious served straightaway or chilled overnight. If serving hot, serve with a pour of double (heavy) cream.

balancing elements
prunes (subtly sour)
brandy (subtly bitter)
salt

Far Breton, where have you been all my life? Cousin of the cherry clafoutis, this is a French dessert that involves a rich, dense custard set around jammy, boozy prunes. Somehow it took me over three decades on this planet to discover it – don't let it take you even a fraction of that time to make it: it is so simple and so very good.

Serves 6–8

for the custard
500ml (17fl oz/generous
    2 cups) whole milk
2 eggs
2 egg yolks, at room temperature
90g (3oz/½ cup)
    caster (superfine) sugar
75g (3oz) melted butter, cooled,
    plus extra for greasing
¾ tsp fine sea salt
1 tsp vanilla bean paste
70g (2¾oz/generous ½ cup)
    plain (all-purpose) flour
1 tbsp demerara (turbinado) sugar,
    plus extra to sprinkle on at the end

for the prunes
150g (5oz) pitted prunes
50ml (2fl oz/3 tbsp plus 1 tsp)
    Armagnac or dark rum,
    Cognac or brandy
double (heavy) cream, to serve

equipment
blender
23cm (9in) round baking dish
    (or similar)

1 Make the custard by adding all the ingredients, except the demerara sugar, to a blender and blitzing briefly until mostly smooth and lump-free. Refrigerate for 1 hour.

2 In a small saucepan, warm the prunes with the Armagnac over a medium heat, stirring occasionally, until most of the liquid is absorbed, around 8–10 minutes. Cover, remove from the heat and leave to cool.

3 Preheat the oven to 180°C fan/200°C/400°F/gas 6. Grease the baking dish with softened butter, then sprinkle with the tablespoon of demerara sugar and dot around the cooled prunes (keep the soaking liquid).

4 Whisk the custard mix briefly, adding any leftover Armagnac from the prunes, then pour into the prepared baking dish. Bake in the oven until risen, lightly golden on top and firm to the touch, around 30 minutes. Sprinkle over some extra demerara sugar, then leave to cool for around 20–30 minutes (the prunes get very hot!). Slice to serve warm, or store in the fridge overnight and serve the next day.

Tip Most batters – whether for Yorkshire puddings, crêpes, blinis, farinata, etc. – benefit from some resting time before cooking. This allows the flour to properly hydrate. See also: Crêpes with Plantain + Rum Caramel (page 68), Russian Honey (Crêpe) Cake (page 168) and Currant Dutch Baby with Honeyed Ricotta (page 192).

black
tea
eccles
cakes

The pie dough for these is best made the day before, as it needs several hours' rest in the fridge (alternatively, you could use store-bought puff pastry).

balancing elements
currants (sour)
black tea (subtly bitter)
orange zest (subtly bitter), light muscovado (subtle acidity)
Lancashire cheese (salty, umami)

I've heard Eccles cakes described as a 'sort of currant sandwich' and such a humble description feels appropriate for what is a northern English treat (Northerners are, by definition, self-effacing and no nonsense!). The ready-made versions that you can get in the supermarket are, I promise you, not worth your time – but a homemade Eccles cake? It's a thing of joy, my friends. And truly delicious served with a slice of Lancashire cheese (in the style of St. John restaurant).

Makes 8–10

1 quantity of Pie Dough
   (see page 228)
1 tbsp demerara
   (turbinado) sugar
1 Earl Grey teabag
1 egg, for egg wash

for the filling
120g (4½oz/scant 1 cup) currants,
   soaked in 1 mug (200ml/7fl oz)
   double-strength Earl Grey tea
50g (2oz/3 tbsp) mixed peel
zest of 1 small orange
30g (1oz) fridge-cold
   butter, grated
75g (3oz/generous ¼ cup) light
   muscovado (or soft light
   brown) sugar
¾ tsp ground nutmeg
½ tsp allspice
¼ tsp fine sea salt

equipment
spice blender (or pestle and mortar)
pastry brush
9cm (3½in) cookie cutter (ideal,
   not essential)

1 Drain the currants from the tea and add to a medium bowl along with the rest of the filling ingredients. Stir together until the sugar has started to dissolve.

2 Roll out your pie dough to 4mm (¼in) thick, then cut out rounds about 9cm (3¾in) in diameter. Put a teaspoon of filling in the centre of each round, dampen the edges with water and bring them together in the middle, pressing together to seal. Place on a lined baking tray, smooth side up, and use a rolling pin to very gently flatten them out slightly. Place in the fridge to chill for 1 hour.

3 Meanwhile, briefly blitz together the demerara sugar and leaves from the tea bag in a spice blender (or similar) to create a coarse, flavoured sugar.

4 Preheat the oven to 200°C fan/220°C/425°F/gas 7 shortly before you're planning to bake the Eccles cakes.

5 Brush the Eccles cakes with the beaten egg, then sprinkle with the black tea sugar. Place in the oven and turn the heat down to 170°C fan/190°C/375°F/gas 5. Bake until golden, puffed up and the pie dough is cooked on the bottom, around 20 minutes. Remove from the oven and allow to cool before eating.

apple mincemeat filo pie (pastis gascon)

Filo (phyllo) comes in all shapes and sizes, so take the quantity below as a rough guide.

If you're in a hurry, you can forego lining the dish with filo, and simply pop the scrunched-up sheets on top to form a 'lid'.

This can easily be doubled to fit a larger dish/serve more people.

This is best served with tangy French crème fraîche (or sour cream), but cold double (heavy) cream is also lovely.

balancing elements
lemon juice (sour)
brandy (subtly bitter)
crème fraîche (sour/tangy)

Pastis Gascon is a fundamentally rustic yet flouncy French apple pie that's soft and mildly boozy on the inside (hello, brandy) and shatteringly crisp on the outside from the use of filo pastry. It's the kind of low-fuss, relatively light dessert that is perfect for using up any leftover mincemeat once Christmas has passed.

Serves 3–4

for the filling
1 Bramley cooking apple, peeled, quartered and cored
2 Pink Lady apples, peeled, quartered and cored
juice of ½ lemon
around 140g (4½oz) mincemeat (give or take is fine)
1 tbsp caster (superfine) or granulated sugar, plus extra for sprinkling
3 tbsp Armagnac (or brandy)

to assemble
6–7 filo (phyllo) pastry sheets
85g (3¼oz) butter, melted

to serve
icing (confectioners') sugar
crème fraîche

equipment
30cm (12in) round pie dish (I use a large Falcon enamel serving bowl)

1   Preheat the oven to 170°C fan/190°C/375°F/gas 5. Place a baking tray in the oven to heat up.

2   Thinly slice the apple quarters crossways and place in a medium bowl. Squeeze over the lemon juice, then add the rest of the filling ingredients and toss together.

3   To assemble the pie, cover the filo sheets with a slightly damp dish towel while you work, so that they don't dry out. Brush the pie dish with a thin layer of the melted butter, sprinkle with a teaspoon of sugar, then add a sheet of filo to the bottom of the tin, letting any excess overhang. Brush this filo layer with more butter and sprinkle with more sugar, then place a second sheet of filo over the top, rotating it slightly so that the excess hangs out at a different angle. Repeat with 2 more layers of filo.

4   Fill the pie dish with the apple mincemeat mixture, leaving any excess liquid behind in the bowl.

5   Lay a sheet of filo on your work surface, brush with the melted butter, sprinkle with a teaspoon of sugar and scrunch it up, then arrange it on top of half of the pie (if your sheets are really big, then you may choose to halve them). Repeat with another sheet of filo, placing this on the other half, creating a full pie 'lid' and tucking in any overhang, like a messy bedsheet. Drizzle any remaining melted butter over the top.

6   Place the pie on the preheated baking tray and bake until the pastry is cooked through and golden brown, around 45 minutes. (Check it halfway through the cooking time and turn the oven down to 160°C fan/180°C/350°F/gas 4 if the pastry looks as though it's getting dark quite quickly.)

7   Allow the pie to cool for 15 minutes before serving warm, dusted lightly with icing sugar and with a spoonful of crème fraîche alongside.

date, fennel seed + lemon scones

These require a brief chill in the fridge before baking (or overnight).

Segmenting the scones (rather than punching them out with a round cutter) ensures a better rise and no wastage.

Avoid tough scones by handling the dough as little as possible (the more you handle the dough, the more you develop the gluten in the flour!)

These are delicious served with labneh (or clotted cream) and honey.

balancing elements
lemon zest (bitter)
fennel seeds (herbal/aniseed),
buttermilk (sour/tangy)
labneh (sour/tangy)
salt

The thing that must be understood about scones is that they deserve to be eaten fresh out of the oven. So while you can order a scone at a café, or head for cream tea at a tea room, or even pick up a whole pack of scones from the supermarket, no scone that you could ever buy will live up to the scone that you can make for yourself. This is a fantastic base recipe (adapted from the infamous Tartine Bakery in California) that you can tweak to take it in different flavour directions. Still, the combination of jammy dates, fragrant lemon zest and herbal fennel seeds is a special one that straddles the sweet-savoury divide.

Makes 6 large scones

300g (10½oz/scant 2½ cups)
   plain (all-purpose) flour,
   plus extra for dusting
1½ tsp baking powder
½ tsp bicarbonate of soda
   (baking soda)
50g (2oz/¼ cup) caster (superfine)
   or granulated sugar
1 tsp fine sea salt
2 tsp fennel seeds, lightly crushed
zest of 1 lemon
110g (3¾oz) butter, fridge-cold and
   cut into 1cm (½in) cubes, plus
   20g (¾oz) melted
75g (3oz) Medjool dates,
   pitted and roughly chopped
200ml (7fl oz/generous
   ¾ cup) buttermilk
demerara (turbinado) sugar,
   for sprinkling
labneh (or clotted cream), to serve
honey, to serve

equipment
dough scraper (helpful,
   not essential)

1 Line a baking tray with greaseproof paper (or a silicone baking mat).

2 Whisk together the flour, raising agents, sugar, salt, fennel seeds and lemon zest in a large bowl. Add the cubed butter and use your hands (or a pastry cutter) to rub the butter into the dry ingredients until the mixture has pea-sized lumps of butter. Toss through the chopped dates.

3 Pour in the buttermilk and combine just until the dough starts to come together. At this point, tip the dough onto a floured surface and pat into a circle shape around 3–4cm (1–1½in) thick. Cut the circle into 6 segments and transfer these to the prepared baking tray. Chill in the fridge for 30 minutes (or overnight).

4 Before the end of the chilling time, preheat the oven to 200°C fan/ 220°C/425°F/gas 7.

5 When ready to bake, brush each scone with melted butter, then sprinkle over a little demerara sugar. Bake until the scones are golden on top, around 20 minutes. Allow to cool for 5 minutes, before serving with labneh (or clotted cream) and honey.

Tip To make 'faux' buttermilk, simply combine 100ml (3½fl oz/generous ⅓ cup) whole milk with 2 tbsp fresh lemon juice. See also: Strawberries + Cream Cake (page 76).

hot buttered apples with bay custard

This can easily be halved or doubled.

If you use gluten-free oats, this makes a great coeliac-friendly dessert.

If you fancy a dessert that's on the less sweet side, swap the Pink Lady apples for Granny Smiths.

If you can, do get hold of fresh bay leaves for the custard.

balancing elements
Pink Lady apples (sweet/tart)
apple cider (subtle acidity, subtle bitterness)
bay leaf (herbal/aniseed)
sour cream (sour/tangy)
currants (sweet/tart)

I'm as guilty as the next person for gravitating towards the sexy dessert – you know the ones: a voluptuous tiramisu, a naughty sticky toffee pudding, a decadent chocolate tart. 'Baked fruit', well, frankly it just doesn't hit the same. But can I make a case for these hot buttered apples – a sexy(ish) name for what is essentially baked apples? Sure, they're humble. They're not gonna win any beauty contests. They're not crazy indulgent in the way that we often expect desserts to be. But in the words of Beyoncé: they are COZY – and sometimes that's just what you want.

Serves 4–6

6 Pink Lady apples
15g (½oz) butter, cubed
1 tbsp demerara (turbinado) sugar, for sprinkling
200ml (7 fl oz/generous ¾ cup) apple cider (or warm water), for baking

for the custard
500ml (17fl oz/generous 2 cups) whole milk
10 fresh bay leaves, torn in half
70g (2¾oz/⅓ cup) caster (superfine) sugar
¼ tsp fine sea salt
6 large egg yolks
1 tbsp cornflour (cornstarch)
60g (2¼oz/¼ cup) sour cream

for the filling
75g (3oz) butter, softened
3 tbsp maple syrup
½ tsp ground cinnamon
generous pinch of fine sea salt
30g (1oz/⅓ cup) rolled oats
40g (1½oz/⅓ cup) currants
30g (1oz) marzipan, cut into 5mm (¼in) cubes

equipment
baking dish to fit the apples snugly

1 Start by infusing the milk for the custard. Add the milk, bay leaves, half of the sugar (eyeball it) and the salt to a heavy-based saucepan and heat until steaming. Remove from the heat and leave to infuse for at least 20 minutes (longer is ideal).

2 Core the apples so that they remain closed at the bottom (you want to create a sort of upside-down cone shape in the top), then stand them up, side by side, in a baking dish.

3 Preheat the oven to 170°C fan/190°C/375°F/gas 5.

4 To make the filling, beat together the butter, maple syrup, cinnamon and salt in a bowl, then stir through the oats, currants and cubed marzipan.

5 Stuff the cored apples with the filling, dot over the cubed butter, then sprinkle each with demerara sugar. Pour the apple cider (or warm water) in and around the apples, then bake until the fruit is soft and yielding – after around 50 minutes–1 hour. The apples will be tender at this point, but you can bake them longer if you want them to be softer. Remove from the oven and allow to cool for 5–10 minutes before serving.

6 Meanwhile, around 10 minutes before the apples come out of the oven, start making the custard. Remove the bay leaves then heat the milk back up to steaming. In a separate bowl, whisk together the egg yolks with the remaining sugar and the cornflour until smooth and slightly lightened in colour. Whisk in around a quarter of the hot milk, followed by the rest. Pour the custard back into the saucepan, set over a very gentle heat and stir continuously with a spatula until the mixture thickens and coats the back of a spoon (this is likely to take a good 10–15 minutes). Pour the custard through a sieve into a jug and then cover the top with cling film (plastic wrap) to stop a skin forming. Just before serving, whisk through the sour cream.

7 To serve, pour two-thirds of the warm custard onto a serving platter and arrange the hot buttered apples on top. Pour the rest of the custard into a jug and bring to the table along with the apples. Serve immediately.

simple caribbean black cake

The fruit needs to be cooked and soaked a week before you make the cake.

Caribbean black cake would typically include 'browning' – deeply caramelised sugar – to add depth of flavour, but I swap in blackstrap molasses for ease

This cake will keep for a couple of weeks, and during this time you can continue to 'feed' it with dark rum, if you like.

balancing elements
all the booze (bitter)
currants (sour)
molasses (sour/bitter)
prunes (subtly sour)

I love Christmas and have a deep attachment to almost all the food associated with it – mince pies, Christmas pudding, cranberry sauce, etc. – but the one thing that has never floated my boat is the traditional British Christmas cake. Typically it consists of a fruit cake (dry) topped with a blanket of marzipan (thick, cloying) followed by a layer of white icing (sickly sweet). Which I guess explains why we never make that kind of Christmas cake anymore. Instead, a family recipe for Caribbean black cake is our festive bake of choice, and I promise it'll become yours too, once you try it. Moist, aggressively boozy, sweet but not too sweet – it's a humble cake that involves minimal faff (something we all need at Christmas) and keeps wonderfully for weeks.

Makes 1 x 20cm (8in) cake

350g (12oz/2½ cups) raisins
200g (7oz/generous 1½ cups) currants
150g (5oz) prunes
100g (3½oz/7 tbsp) candied peel
80ml (3fl oz/⅓ cup) dark rum
80ml (3fl oz/⅓ cup) port
80ml (3fl oz/⅓ cup) brandy
80ml (3fl oz/⅓ cup) water
2 tbsp blackstrap molasses
1 tsp ground allspice
½ tsp ground cinnamon
½ tsp ground ginger
½ tsp grated nutmeg
200g (7oz/generous 1½ cups) self-raising flour
½ tsp fine sea salt
200g (7oz/generous 1 cup) light muscovado (or soft light brown) sugar
200g (7oz) butter, softened
4 eggs, at room temperature

equipment
23cm (9in) (or 20cm/8in) non-stick, loose-bottomed or springform cake tin
electric hand mixer

1   Add all the dried fruit, liquids, molasses and spices to a saucepan and bring to a gentle simmer. Cook for 15 minutes or so, giving it an occasional stir – the fruit should look plump and glossy. Allow to cool, then transfer to a sealed container and place in the fridge for a week.

2   When ready to bake, preheat the oven to 140°C fan/160°C/325°F/gas 3. Line the base of your cake tin with greaseproof paper.

3   To make the cake, add the flour, salt, sugar, butter and eggs to a large bowl. Whisk together with an electric hand mixer, just until combined and homogenous. Next, fold in the soaked fruit. Pour into the prepared cake tin and place on the middle shelf in the oven. Bake until an inserted skewer comes out clean – start checking around the 2-hour mark (you can place some greaseproof paper over the top of the cake if it's browning too quickly).

4   Allow to cool for around 30 minutes in the tin before turning out onto a wire rack to cool completely. Store in a covered container at room temperature – you can 'feed' the cake with extra rum or brandy over several days, if you like. I certainly like to.

sticky figgy pudding with walnut butterscotch

The butterscotch can be made up to 2 days in advance and gently reheated to serve.

balancing elements
walnuts (subtly bitter)
brown butter (subtle umami)
crème fraîche (sour/tangy)
light muscovado (subtle acidity)

In the UK we sometimes call Christmas pudding 'figgy pudding' but that's not what we're dealing with here. Instead, think of this as a sticky toffee pudding-adjacent affair where the dates have been replaced by dried figs. It's a sticky, caramelised, naughty kinda pudding – one for the sweet-toothed among us – but the tangy crème fraîche and subtly bitter walnuts in the sauce keep the sweetness just about in check. Serve with cold double (heavy) cream.

Serves 9, generously

100g (3½oz) butter
150g (5oz) dried figs, stalks removed and roughly chopped
⅛ tsp bicarbonate of soda (baking soda)
100ml (3½fl oz/generous ⅓ cup) water
90g (3¼oz/scant ½ cup) light muscovado (or light brown) sugar
175g (6oz/generous 1¼ cups) self-raising flour
1 tsp baking powder
½ tsp ground cinnamon
¼ tsp fine sea salt
2 eggs
75ml (2½fl oz/scant ⅓ cup) whole milk
1 tsp vanilla bean paste
double (heavy) cream, to serve

for the sauce
150g (5oz) butter
300g (10½oz/generous 1½ cups) light muscovado (or soft light brown) sugar
250ml (8½fl oz/generous 1 cup) double (heavy) cream
½ tsp flaky sea salt
75g (3oz/generous ¼ cup) crème fraîche
60g (2¼oz) walnuts, chopped

equipment
23cm (9in) square non-stick, loose-bottomed baking tin (or similar)

1 Preheat the oven to 160°C fan/180°C/350°F/gas 4 and line the base of your tin with greaseproof paper.

2 Brown the butter In a saucepan over a medium heat, taking it as far as you can without burning it – this usually takes 10–15 minutes.

3 Place the dried figs, bicarb and 100ml of water in a separate saucepan, bring to the boil, then simmer for 5 minutes. Use a fork to mash the figs into a rough paste and set aside.

4 Whisk together the brown sugar, flour, baking powder, ground cinnamon and salt in a medium–large mixing bowl, using your hands to break up any lumps of sugar.

5 In a separate jug or bowl, whisk together the eggs, browned butter, milk, vanilla and mashed figs. Add this to the dry ingredients and whisk just until you have a homogenous batter.

6 Pour the mixture into your prepared tin and bake until an inserted skewer comes out clean, around 30 minutes.

7 Meanwhile, make the sauce by combining the butter and brown sugar in a small saucepan. Set over a low heat and stir every so often until the butter has melted and the sugar has dissolved. Add the cream and salt, bring briefly to a simmer, then remove from the heat and whisk in the crème fraîche. Stir through the chopped walnuts.

8 As soon as the pudding is out of the oven, prick it all over with a cocktail stick and pour a quarter of the sauce over, spreading it to the edges. Place a lid on the pan with the sauce to keep it warm, and set the pudding aside for 20 minutes or so. Serve slabs of the pudding with additional sauce and cold double cream.

Tip Adding browned butter to cakes is a great way of adding depth of flavour and works especially well with autumnal and winter flavours – think caramel, nuts and sweet spices. See also: Brown Butter, Pear + Hazelnut Cake (page 176) and Toasted ANZAC Biscuits (page 124).

sweetness in a savoury world

For quite some time, at least in the UK, there's been a relatively firm sweet-savoury divide. Sweet and savoury were expected to stay firmly in their lanes, occupying different courses on the menu. And we categorised each other's food tastes this way, too: you were either a savoury or sweet person, you preferred either dessert or the cheese plate. Then salted caramel landed, and the distinction started to blur. Today you might reasonably identify as a 'sweet 'n' salty' kinda person. And I reckon that's as it should be – because just as your desserts ought to include salt, so it is important to consider sweetness in savoury cooking.

We've not always had such polarised tastes. In the Middle Ages, food was not divided and served by flavour – sweet courses would be interspersed throughout a banquet and dishes such as honeyed herb fritters would straddle the sweet-savoury divide. A medieval blancmange (a dish we know of today as a sweet milk custard, set like a jelly) featured capon (a type of poultry), blanched almonds, rice, lard, salt and sugar: a jarring mix of sugar alongside meat. In this way, sweetness was considered a seasoning – no different to salt, or a pinch of spice. All things said, I'm not advocating for a return to a medieval view of sweetness (hard pass on that blancmange, thanks) but there *is* merit in the inclusion of sweet flavours in savoury dishes, and it's something we ought to consider when cooking.

A good place to start is with sweet vegetables, of which there are plenty: butternut squash, sweet potato, carrots, parsnips. Their use can counterbalance more strongly savoury main meals, such as umami-rich stews. Or they can be a star in their own right, particularly suited to contrasting flavours – there's a reason that sweet potatoes love lime, carrots love spices, and parsnips love miso. Then there's fresh fruit, which plays off beautifully against strong salty flavours (think melon and Parma ham; or pears and blue cheese, see page 186) as well as milder, creamy cheeses (peaches love mozzarella and burrata, see page 210). Often these sorts of dishes are the purest representation of how balancing the tastes can yield the most delicious results. In this regard, salads can be a particularly useful and easy way to experiment with flavours, with clear components that can each speak to salty/sweet/sour/bitter/umami flavours. Transitioning into the realm of dried or cooked fruit, it is easy to recognise that a jammy chutney enhances a plate of salty, umami cheese; or the importance of cranberry sauce on the Christmas table (and apple sauce with roast pork, for that matter); or how sticky prunes can meld beautifully with lamb or beef to create a fragrant tagine.

The symphony of sugar and salt has existed in many cultures for centuries: from the tagines of Morocco to the ripe plantains that are a staple in south American and Caribbean cooking. From Persian cuisine – where dried fruits and fruit-based molasses feature – to the use of palm sugar as seasoning in Thai dishes. From India, where sweet chutneys feature frequently and dishes descended from the Mughal Empire employ plenty of sweet fruits, to the sweet and sour dishes of China (particularly across the eastern regions, such as Jiangsu and Guangdong). Even in America, sweet-savoury favourites have been common for a good while: smoked brisket served with sweet BBQ sauce; the cornbread always present at potlucks in the southern states; the ubiquity of a ham and pineapple pizza (which originated in Canada). Somehow, it felt like the UK was out of the loop. Still, a greater awareness today about introducing both harmony and contrast into our food – which is where considering the five tastes comes in handy – has made for more exciting eating, and a more vibrant gastronomic scene, too.

Beyond balancing the five tastes, it's important to think of sugar as a tool in your savoury cooking. It stimulates your taste buds, it's a way of seasoning food (don't just salt your meat, sugar it a bit, too – trust me) and it's a remedy for food that is too salty, sour or spicy (think of the way that sweet mango chutney soothes a chilli-heavy curry). When making a Thai green curry your seasoning arsenal includes palm sugar, not just fish sauce, fresh lime juice and chilli. You can make a ragu with beef stock, but it's definitely better and more balanced in flavour when subtly sweet milk joins the party. Pickles require both sugar *and* salt to sing. In fact, I'll let you in on a secret: a gastrique – a caramel let down with vinegar – is often used by professional chefs to season sauces, and the reason it's so effective is that it offers up the magic combination of sugar and acid (white balsamic vinegar is a ready-made approximation). Combined with salt, these three make up what I call the holy trinity of seasoning – a key principle for anyone looking to enhance the flavour of their food.

burnt peach + burrata with hot sauce dressing

You want peaches that are not too ripe and soft, otherwise they'll fall apart when you grill them.

This is best served with slices of griddled sourdough for scooping everything up.

The heat of your dressing will depend on the heat of your hot sauce, so do taste it before deciding how much to use to dress your salad.

sweet elements
peaches
burrata

Peaches and cream aren't just a great combination in desserts – it's a pairing that carries over seamlessly into the savoury world. This is a luscious and fun salad, perfect for bright summer days.

Serves 2 (or 4 as part of a wider spread)

2 small peaches, pitted, halved and each half cut into 3
1 tbsp olive oil
1 x 150g (5oz) ball of burrata
2 slices of prosciutto (or Parma ham), each roughly torn in half
10 Thai basil (or standard basil) leaves
fine sea salt
black pepper

for the hot sauce dressing
1½ tsp hot sauce
1 tbsp extra-virgin olive oil
1 tsp rice vinegar
1 tsp runny honey
pinch of fine sea salt

equipment
medium–large grill pan (or frying pan/skillet)

1   Set the grill pan over a high heat and allow to get hot for a few minutes. Brush the peaches with a little olive oil and place them on the hot grill pan, cut sides down. Allow to cook without disturbing for 4–5 minutes, then flip over and cook on the other cut sides. Once cooked, remove the peaches from the pan and allow to cool.

2   While the peaches are cooking, make the dressing by whisking all the ingredients together until the honey has dissolved.

3   Compile your salad: place the burrata on a serving platter and pierce with a small sharp knife, opening it up and spreading it across the plate a little. Arrange the grilled peach wedges over the top, then nestle the prosciutto in and among the items on the plate. Drizzle over the dressing, then scatter over the basil leaves and season with salt and pepper.

sweetness in a savoury world

rosemary milk buns

Do check that your yeast is in date before starting the process!

You could swap the rosemary for any other hard herb (e.g. thyme).

sweet elements
milk
honey

Nothing pleases guests more than freshly baked bread, but freshly baked bread rolls? Well, that's comfortably into domestic goddess territory. And yet, I have to tell you that while these are exceptionally good – light, impossibly fluffy, golden and beautifully glossy from the rosemary and honey-butter glaze – they are also incredibly easy to make. Loosely based on Hokkaido milk bread from Japan, the milk tenderises the dough, contributing to the rolls' plush texture. Perfect for any lunch, dinner or picnic.

Makes 15

240ml (8fl oz/1 cup) whole milk
7g (¼oz) active dry yeast
30g (1oz/2½ tbsp) caster (superfine) or granulated sugar
1 large egg
50g (2oz) butter, at room temperature
1¼ tsp fine sea salt
410g (14oz/3 cups plus 3 tbsp) strong white bread flour
3 tbsp finely chopped rosemary

for the glaze
25g (1oz) slightly salted butter
2 sprigs of rosemary
1 tbsp honey

equipment
stand mixer with dough hook attachment
(23 x 33cm (9 x 13in) baking tray, approx. 5cm (2in) high, lined with greaseproof paper
dough scraper (helpful, not essential)
temperature probe (helpful, not essential)
pastry brush

1 Heat the milk to around 40°C (104°F) (if you don't have a temperature probe, briefly heat it in a pan until it's warm to the touch), then pour into the mixing bowl of the stand mixer, add the yeast and 15g (½oz/ 1 heaped tbsp) of the sugar, then cover and set aside for 5–10 minutes. After this time, the mixture should be bubbly and foamy.

2 Add the remaining sugar, egg, butter (cut into 4 pieces), salt and 250g (9oz/2 cups) of the flour. Mix for a minute until combined, scraping down the sides. Add the remaining flour and chopped rosemary, then knead the mixture until you can successfully perform the windowpane test (see page 50), around 10 minutes. Cover the bowl and set aside to prove until doubled in size, around 1–2 hours (see tip).

3 After the dough has risen, punch it down to deflate it, then divide the mix into even-sized pieces (I eyeball this, although you could weigh the pieces, if you like). Form each piece into a ball (I tuck all the sides into the centre, turn the piece over so that the 'joins' are underneath, then I cup my hand over the dough ball and rotate in an anticlockwise direction to create some tension against the work surface that will encourage the dough to tighten into a ball – it might be best to view an online tutorial for this!). Place the dough balls on the lined baking tray, evenly spaced, then cover with cling film (plastic wrap) and set aside to rise again, around 1–2 hours (there should no longer be any gaps between the bread rolls).

4 Preheat the oven to 180°C fan/200°C/400°F/gas 6.

5 Bake the bread rolls until risen and golden, around 20 minutes. Remove from the oven and set aside to cool slightly.

6 Meanwhile, make the glaze by combining all the ingredients in a small saucepan and heating up until the butter is mildly sizzling. Turn the heat off and allow the rosemary to infuse for a couple of minutes before using a pastry brush to glaze the tops of the rolls. Serve them warm.

Tip To create a reliable environment to prove dough, turn your oven on for exactly 60 seconds, then turn it off – this will create a perfectly warm environment. See also: Cardamom Brioche Loaf (page 50), Rum + Grapefruit Babas (page 46) and Bee Sting Cake (page 164).

roasted plantain, chickpea + dill salad

When picking out your plantain, opt for fruit that is black and has a soft, squishy texture when squeezed.

Since this is a salad (rather than a stew or curry), it pays to buy jarred chickpeas, as they are infinitely more delicious than the canned versions and you'll notice it here. I love the ones by Navarrico and Bold Bean Co.

sweet elements
plantain
maple syrup

This recipe makes a nice change from the more predictable ways of cooking plantain (fries, tostones, etc.). The flavours are earthy and bright, and the beans ensure this has enough substance to work as a sustaining lunch – though it's also great alongside chicken. The starchy beans make the perfect base for the sweet plantain and zingy dressing. This recipe is adapted from Yewande Komolafe, a New York-based chef and recipe developer of Nigerian heritage.

Serves 3-4

2 very ripe plantain
1 tbsp olive oil
¼ tsp flaky sea salt
240g (8½oz/1¾ cups) cooked chickpeas (garbanzo beans)
1 ripe avocado, cubed
1 little gem lettuce, leaves separated
1 spring onion (scallion), finely sliced
10g (¼oz) dill, large stems removed
10g (¼oz) coriander (cilantro), leaves picked
freshly ground black pepper
extra-virgin olive oil, to serve

for the dressing
zest and juice of 1 small lime
2 tbsp olive oil, plus more for drizzling
2 tsp freshly grated ginger
½ small garlic clove, grated
½ tbsp maple syrup

1 Preheat the oven to 220°C fan/240°C/475°F/gas 9.

2 Make the dressing by combining all the ingredients in a jar and shaking until emulsified.

3 Next, prepare the plantain. Trim the ends off, then score the skin down two sides with a small knife, taking care to avoid piercing the flesh. Peel the skin away. Slice the plantain in half lengthways, then each piece in half again – you should have 8 pieces in total. Add to a lined baking tray, drizzle over the olive oil and turn the pieces in it so that they're coated. Season with the salt and some pepper. Bake for 15–20 minutes, flipping halfway through, until deeply golden.

4 While the plantain is in the oven, assemble the rest of the salad: toss together the chickpeas, avocado and little gem leaves with the dressing.

5 To plate, add the chickpea mix to a serving platter, then top with the roasted plantain and sprinkle over the spring onion and herbs. Season with a few grindings of black pepper and drizzle over some extra-virgin olive oil. Serve immediately – I personally really enjoy plantain when it's still hot!

iranian
fried eggs
with dates

sweet element
dates

*I am indebted to Bobak (@bobakcooks) for teaching me how
to make this Iranian breakfast dish, tokhme-morgh va khorma.
If you've never tasted this before, it might be hard to get your head
around the idea of combining something so quintessentially savoury
(a fried egg) with the sweetest of sweet things (dates). I can tell
you: it's a revelation.*

Serves 1-2

1 tbsp butter
2–3 Medjool dates,
   halved and pitted
¼–½ tsp ground cinnamon,
   to taste
2 eggs
2 slices of buttered toast,
   to serve

1 Place a non-stick frying pan (skillet) over a medium heat. Once hot,
   add the butter and allow it to melt and start to foam a little. Add the
   dates and cinnamon, and allow them to fry for a couple of minutes.
   Crack in the eggs among the dates, then cook until the whites are
   cooked and opaque, and the yolks are still runny inside.

2 Transfer the eggs and dates to the buttered toast and eat immediately.

focaccia with strawberries + fennel seeds

This recipe doesn't require huge amounts of hands-on work (it's practically no-knead), but it does require time – including, ideally, 24 hours in the fridge.

Speaking of no-knead, I do encourage you to carry out some folds, which are a very simple way of adding some structure to the dough – but if you are short on time, you could skip these and still get a decent result.

sweet element
strawberries

Three things make this the best focaccia dough: cold fermentation (which means slower fermentation, and therefore better flavour), high hydration (which equals lightness and bubbles) and the use of a brine (even more flavour). But beyond the light, airy, pillowy focaccia that this recipe will yield, there's the slightly unusual addition of strawberries and fennel seeds. Strawberries and tomatoes share aroma compounds in common, so maybe it's helpful to think of this as sitting somewhere between a tomato focaccia and a grape focaccia: slightly sweet, slightly savoury, very moreish.

Serves 8–10

425ml (14½fl oz/1¾ cups) lukewarm water (see tip)
6g (¼oz/2 tsp) active dry yeast
1 tbsp caster (superfine) sugar
500g (1lb 2oz/4 cups) strong white bread flour
1½ tsp fine sea salt
5 tbsp extra-virgin olive oil, plus extra for drizzling
semolina/fine cornmeal, for dusting the baking tray
200g (7oz) strawberries, hulled and quartered
2 tsp fennel seeds

for the brine
80ml (3fl oz/⅓ cup) water
1 tsp fine sea salt

equipment
23 x 33cm (9 x 13in) baking tray with a 3–4cm (1–1½in) lip

1   Combine half of the water with the yeast and sugar, cover and leave for 5 minutes until the mixture has bubbled up and become foamy.

2   Separately, combine the flour and salt together in a large bowl.

3   Create a well in the middle of the flour mixture, then pour in the yeast mixture, along with the rest of the water. Use a spoon or your hands to bring the dough together into a craggy ball. Rub the surface of the dough lightly with 3 tablespoons of the olive oil, then cover the bowl with cling film (plastic wrap) and place in the refrigerator overnight.

4   The next morning, remove the bowl from the fridge and perform a few folds on the dough – essentially pulling the dough out from underneath and folding it over the top, then turning the bowl 90 degrees and repeating three times. Turn the dough over in the bowl, pour over another tablespoon of olive oil, re-cover with cling film, then set aside. Repeat the folds two to three more times, every hour or so.

5   Push a piece of greaseproof paper into the baking tin, then dust the base with semolina. Turn the dough out into the tin, rub over another tablespoon of olive oil and use your fingers to gently stretch the dough to the edges of the baking tray. Cover with cling film and leave to rise one last time, around an hour.

6   Preheat the oven to 220°C fan/240°C/475°F/gas 9 and place an upturned baking tray (or baking stone) into the oven to heat up.

7   Meanwhile, scatter the strawberries and fennel seeds over the focaccia and use your fingers to press them deep into the dough (if they're too exposed they might burn). Finally, combine the water and salt to make the brine and pour this evenly over the bread. Transfer to the oven, placing the baking tin on top of the upturned tray. Bake until puffed up and deeply golden on top, around 20–25 minutes. Allow the focaccia to cool for 10 minutes before cutting and serving.

Tip For perfectly lukewarm water without a temperature probe, combine one third boiling water with two thirds cold water – this will land you with water that's around the 35°C (95°F) mark.

pear, gorgonzola + walnut potato-crusted quiche

This recipe works best if you have a mandoline for slicing the potatoes.

This is an ideal solution if you are catering for someone who is gluten-free.

sweet elements
pear
milk

A potato-crusted quiche is a slightly fiddly but very fun version of a quiche that caters brilliantly to anyone who is gluten-free. The base quiche custard in this recipe is a trusty Tartine recipe that has the requisite amount of tartness from crème fraîche to offer the right flavour balance. Meanwhile, the combination of sweet pear, umami blue cheese and bitter walnuts is a well-worn one – and for good reason!

Serves 6–8

for the potato crust
400g (14oz) Maris Piper potatoes
2–3 tbsp olive oil
¼ tsp fine sea salt

for the filling
5 eggs
40g (1½oz/⅓ cup) plain (all-purpose) flour
½ tsp fine sea salt
200ml (7fl oz/generous ¾ cup) crème fraîche
240ml (8fl oz/1 cup) whole milk
freshly ground black pepper
75g (3oz) gorgonzola (or similar)
50g (2oz) walnuts, toasted and roughly chopped
2 small pears, halved, cored and sliced
2 tsp fresh thyme leaves

equipment
mandoline
quiche pan or pie dish

1   Preheat the oven to 180°C fan/200°C/400°F/gas 6.

2   Use a mandoline to thinly slice the potatoes 3mm (⅛in) thick. Place them in a bowl and coat with the olive oil and salt. Line the quiche pan with the potatoes, overlapping them as you go and ensuring that the edges stick up above the rim of your dish. Place on a baking tray in the oven and bake for 20–30 minutes.

3   While the potato crust is baking, make the filling by whisking together the eggs, flour and salt. Combine the crème fraîche and whole milk in a separate bowl and strain the egg mixture through a sieve into the crème fraîche mixture. Whisk everything together, add several grindings of black pepper, then stir in the cheese.

4   Remove the potato crust from the oven and scatter over the walnuts. Pour the cheese mix into the potato crust, then top with the pear slices and thyme leaves. Return to the oven and bake for 40 minutes until the quiche is mostly set but still slightly wobbly in the middle.

5   Allow to cool for 30 minutes before slicing. It can be served warm or at room temperature.

plt
(prawn
lettuce
tomato)

sweet elements
prawns
coconut

I've never been the biggest fan of bacon (or a BLT), but prawns?
I can get on board with prawns – especially when they're encrusted
in cornflakes and coconut. Enter the PLT: the sandwich you never knew
you needed. Golden-crusted prawns are served up in a bun with lettuce,
tomato and a little pimped-up mayonnaise.

Serves 4

for the pimped chive aioli
½ very small garlic clove, grated
5g (¼oz) chives, finely chopped
   (I find scissors easiest for this)
zest and juice of ½ lime
8 tbsp good-quality mayonnaise
   (I like Kewpie)
pinch of fine sea salt

for the coconut prawns
40g (1½oz/5 tbsp) plain
   (all-purpose) flour
½ tsp paprika
1 tsp fine sea salt
2 eggs
4 tbsp water
40g (1½oz/1½ cups) cornflakes
40g (1½oz/½ cup) desiccated
   (unsweetened shredded)
   coconut
450g (1lb) frozen raw and peeled
   jumbo king prawns, defrosted
vegetable oil, for frying

for the sandwich
4 brioche buns
8 little gem leaves
1–2 ripe tomatoes, thickly sliced

equipment
temperature probe
   (helpful, not essential)

1 Make the aioli first by stirring together all the ingredients in a bowl.

2 In a small bowl, mix together the flour, paprika and salt. In another small bowl, beat the eggs with the measured water. In a third bowl, crush the cornflakes in your hand until very fine and combine with the coconut. Dip each prawn first into the flour mixture, then into the egg, and finally into the coconut crumbs. Set aside on a plate.

3 In a deep frying pan (skillet) or wok, pour in enough oil to come about 3cm (1in) up the sides. Heat over a medium heat until the oil reaches 180°C (350°F), or a cube of bread turns golden in seconds. Carefully lower the prawns into the hot oil and fry, in batches, for 1–2 minutes until golden and crisp. Remove using a slotted spoon and drain on a piece of kitchen paper.

4 To assemble the sandwich, lightly toast the buns and spread a little aioli on each side. Layer up with a lettuce leaf, a big pile of prawns, a slice of tomato and another lettuce leaf. Serve immediately

prune + thyme sausage rolls

I find it easiest to make the sausage filling the day before and chill it overnight.

Homemade pastry makes these knockout (if making the pie dough from scratch, this is best done the day before), but you could use store-bought puff pastry in a pinch – Jus-Rol works really well here.

sweet element
prunes

The addition of sweet prunes to the deep, umami flavour of a sausage roll is a match made in (picnic) heaven.

Makes 10-12

around 400g (14oz) meat from high-quality sausages, removed from their casings
1 tbsp wholegrain mustard
70g (3oz) prunes, roughly chopped
4 sage leaves, finely chopped
1½ tsp fennel seeds
1 tsp dried oregano
freshly ground black pepper
1 quantity of Pie Dough (see page 228) (or store-bought puff pastry)
1 egg, beaten, for egg wash
1 tbsp nigella seeds

1   Combine the sausage meat, mustard, prunes, sage, fennel seeds, oregano and a generous amount of black pepper in a large bowl and mix well by hand. Chill for 1–2 hours (or overnight).

2   Preheat the oven to 200°C fan/220°C/425°F/gas 7 and line a baking tray with greaseproof paper.

3   Roll out the pie dough into a large square, about 30 x 30cm (12 x 12in). Cut the square in half to give you two pieces, 15 x 30cm (6 x 12in).

4   Divide the filling in half and shape each into a sausage shape, roughly the length of the pastry pieces (30cm/12in). Place each one in the centre of the pastry rectangles, then brush the bottom long edges of the pastry with egg wash. Pull the top edges of the pastry over the sausage meat so that they meet the bottom edges, then use the tines of a fork to seal the pastry edges together.

5   Use a serrated bread knife to cut each sausage roll into 5–6 pieces, then transfer to the prepared baking tray, ensuring they're well spaced. Brush each sausage roll with egg wash and sprinkle with the nigella seeds. Bake for 25–30 minutes until deeply golden and the sausage meat is cooked through.

6   Serve either warm or cold, with your condiment of choice.

'any leaf' salad with buttermilk-maple dressing

If you don't have Kewpie mayonnaise, simply use normal mayonnaise and add a little extra vinegar.

The dressing will keep in the fridge for up to 3 days.

sweet element
maple syrup

This is, quite simply, a really excellent dressing that is perfect for salads or slaws. The tang of the buttermilk, the richness of mayonnaise, the subtle allium heat of chives and the sweetness of maple syrup balance perfectly. And the sweetness of the maple syrup becomes especially welcome when paired with crisp bitter leaves.

Serves 2–3

300g (10½oz) sturdy salad leaves (e.g. little gem, chicory, radicchio, etc.) – or a mix of sturdy salad leaves and thinly sliced, fresh, crunchy veg (e.g. celery, fennel)
5g (⅙oz) chives, finely sliced, to garnish

for the dressing
120ml (4fl oz/½ cup) buttermilk
80g (3oz/6 tbsp) Kewpie mayonnaise
1 tbsp apple cider vinegar
1–2 tbsp maple syrup, to taste
5g (⅙oz) chives, finely sliced
4 generous pinches of fine sea salt
lots of freshly ground black pepper

1 To make the dressing, whisk all the ingredients together and adjust the seasoning to taste.

2 Transfer three quarters of the dressing to a large salad bowl, then tumble in the leaves and toss to coat. Add more dressing, if you like. Garnish with the chives and serve immediately.

sweetness in a savoury world

extras

pie
dough

Don't be intimated by this: pie dough is very rewarding to make, not to mention head and shoulders above anything you could buy. I am indebted to Nicola Lamb for the technique here and I will repeat her advice, too: the key when making pie dough is not to panic, okay? It will seem too dry and a bit of a craggy mess at first, but it will all come together after a few folds and a good rest in the fridge (minimum 4 hours). Trust the process.

**Makes enough for 1 pie
or galette**

60ml (2fl oz/¼ cup) ice-cold water,
plus extra as needed
60ml (2fl oz/¼ cup) sour cream
250g (9oz/2 cups) plain
(all-purpose) flour, plus extra
for rolling out, if needed
25g (1oz/2 tbsp) caster
(superfine) sugar
1 tsp flaky sea salt
185g (6½oz) butter, fridge-cold and
cut into 1.5cm (¾in) cubes

equipment
dough scraper (helpful,
not essential)

1   In a small jug, whisk together the water and sour cream, then place in the fridge.

2   In a large bowl, briefly whisk together the flour, sugar and salt. Add the cubes of butter and toss to coat (this helps to protect the butter from the warmth of your hands). Squish the butter into flat pieces, one by one.

3   Pour in the cold cream mixture and squish the dough together. As soon as it's vaguely coming together (it will still be a bit all over the place), tip the dough onto your work surface and squash everything together as best you can. Roll out the dough, adding flour if you need to. You'll see the chunks of butter start to turn into long thin pieces.

4   Roll the dough into a long rectangle (it should be 2–3 times longer than it is wide), then use the dough scraper (or the side of the rolling pin) to nudge the pastry back into a neat shape. Place any dry bits that won't stick into the middle of the rectangle. Ease the dough scraper under the top third of the rectangle of pastry and flip it over into the middle. Use the dough scraper to fold the remaining bottom third of the pastry over the top of the already folded section so that you have a neat rectangular block comprised of three layers. This process is called a 'single turn'.

5   Turn the dough 90 degrees and repeat the above process, performing two more 'single turns' (three single turns in total). The dough should become more homogenous as you do this, and you'll see streaks of butter start to develop in the dough, like marble.

6   Wrap the dough in cling film (plastic wrap) and place in the fridge for at least 4 hours (or overnight) to firm up.

Tip A dough scraper is a multi-tasking hero in the kitchen. Not only is it useful when working with doughs, but it also enables you to transport large quantities of prepped veg from cutting board to stove, and is useful for cleaning your surfaces once you've finished cooking.

sweet
pastry

This pastry needs a minimum
of 2 hours in the fridge to rest,
but it is easier to work with after
an overnight stint in the fridge.

I often double this recipe and put
half in the freezer to save myself
time in future

**Makes enough for 1 x 20cm (8in)
or 23cm (9in) tart**

175g (6oz/scant 1½ cups) plain
   (all-purpose) flour
100g (3½oz) butter, fridge-cold,
   cut into large cubes
¼ tsp fine sea salt
25g (1oz/scant ¼ cup) icing
   (confectioners') sugar
1 egg yolk

equipment
food processor

1 Pulse the flour, butter and salt in the food processor until the texture
   of fine breadcrumbs (alternatively, use the tips of your fingers to rub the
   butter into the flour, then stir through the salt). Add the icing sugar and
   pulse a couple of times to disperse evenly, then add the egg yolk
   and pulse until a ball forms (if after a minute or so it hasn't come
   together add a teaspoon of the egg white leftover from the yolk).

2 Turn the dough out onto a piece of cling film (plastic wrap), wrap it up
   and store in the fridge for at least 2 hours before using (ideally overnight).

index

A

B